COMPREHENSIVE RESEARCH
AND STUDY GUIDE

W.S. Merwin

BLOOM'S
MAJOR
POETS

EDITED AND WITH AN INTRODUCTION
BY HAROLD BLOOM

CURRENTLY AVAILABLE

BLOOM'S MAJOR POETS

Maya Angelou
John Ashbery
Elizabeth Bishop
William Blake
Gwendolyn Brooks
Robert Browning
Geoffrey Chaucer
Sameul Taylor Coleridge
Hart Crane
E.E. Cummings
Dante
Emily Dickinson
John Donne
H.D.
Thomas Hardy
Seamus Heaney
A.E. Housman
T.S. Eliot
Robert Frost
Seamus Heaney
Homer
Langston Hughes
John Keats
W.S. Merwin
John Milton
Marianne Moore
Sylvia Plath
Edgar Allan Poe
Poets of World War I
Christina Rossetti
Wallace Stevens
Mark Strand
Shakespeare's Poems & Sonnets
Percy Shelley
Allen Tate
Alfred, Lord Tennyson
Walt Whitman
William Carlos Williams
William Wordsworth
William Butler Yeats

COMPREHENSIVE RESEARCH
AND STUDY GUIDE

W.S.
Merwin

CHELSEA HOUSE
PUBLISHERS

A Haights Cross Communications Company

Philadelphia

BLOOM'S
MAJOR
POETS

EDITED AND WITH AN INTRODUCTION
BY HAROLD BLOOM

Library of Congress Cataloging-in-Publication Data

W.S. Merwin / [edited and with an introduction by] Harold Bloom.
    p. cm. — (Bloom's major poets)
  Includes bibliographical references and index.
  ISBN 0-7910-7888-4
  1. Merwin, W. S. (William Stanley), 1927—-Criticism and
interpretation. I. Bloom, Harold. II. Series.
  PS3563.E75Z96 2004
  811'.54—dc22

                                                    2004001706

Contributing Editor: Gabriel Welsch

Cover design by Keith Trego

Layout by EJB Publishing Services

CONTENTS

USER'S GUIDE

This volume is designed to present biographical, critical, and bibliographical information on the author and the author's best-known or most important poems. Following Harold Bloom's editor's note and introduction is a concise biography of the author that discusses major life events and important literary accomplishments. A critical analysis of each poem follows, tracing significant themes, patterns, and motifs in the work. As with any study guide, it is recommended that the reader read the poem beforehand and have a copy of the poem being discussed available for quick reference.

A selection of critical extracts, derived from previously published material, follows each thematic analysis. In most cases, these extracts represent the best analysis available from a number of leading critics. Because these extracts are derived from previously published material, they will include the original notations and references when available. Each extract is cited, and readers are encouraged to check the original publication as they continue their research. A bibliography of the author's writings, a list of additional books and articles on the author and their work, and an index of themes and ideas conclude the volume.

ABOUT THE EDITOR

Harold Bloom is Sterling Professor of the Humanities at Yale University. He is the author of over 20 books, and the editor of more than 30 anthologies of literary criticism.

Professor Bloom's works include *Shelley's Mythmaking* (1959), *The Visionary Company* (1961), *Blake's Apocalypse* (1963), *Yeats* (1970), *A Map of Misreading* (1975), *Kabbalah and Criticism* (1975), *Agon: Toward a Theory of Revisionism* (1982), *The American Religion* (1992), *The Western Canon* (1994), and *Omens of Millennium: The Gnosis of Angels, Dreams, and Resurrection* (1996). *The Anxiety of Influence* (1973) sets forth Professor Bloom's provocative theory of the literary relationships between the great writers and their predecessors. His most recent books include *Shakespeare: The Invention of the Human*, a 1998 National Book Award finalist, *How to Read and Why* (2000), *Stories and Poems for Extremely Intelligent Children of All Ages* (2001), *Genius: A Mosaic of One Hundred Exemplary Creative Minds* (2002), and *Hamlet: Poem Unlimited* (2003).

Professor Bloom earned his Ph.D. from Yale University in 1955 and has served on the Yale faculty since then. He is a 1985 MacArthur Foundation Award recipient and served as the Charles Eliot Norton Professor of Poetry at Harvard University in 1987–88. In 1999 he was awarded the prestigious American Academy of Arts and Letters Gold Medal for Criticism. Professor Bloom is the editor of several other Chelsea House series in literary criticism, including BLOOM'S MAJOR SHORT STORY WRITERS, BLOOM'S MAJOR NOVELISTS, BLOOM'S MAJOR DRAMATISTS, BLOOM'S MODERN CRITICAL INTERPRETATIONS, BLOOM'S MODERN CRITICAL VIEWS, BLOOM'S BIOCRITIQUES, BLOOM'S GUIDES, BLOOM'S MAJOR LITERARY CHARACTERS, and BLOOM'S PERIOD STUDIES.

EDITOR'S NOTE

My Introduction centers upon W.S. Merwin's middle phase, particularly the superb volumes: *The Moving Target*, *The Lice*, and *The Carrier of Ladders*. Since I do not discuss any of the five magnificent poems covered in this little volume, the Introduction should supplement the critical views given here, and help illuminate the poet's rather ascetic transcendentalism.

As there are twenty-three critical extracts, I will comment only upon those I myself have found most useful, though everything included seems to me of interpretive value.

On "The Drunk in the Furnace," the poet-critic Richard Howard astutely estimates the cost of confirmation of Merwin's poetic vocation.

"For the Anniversary of My Death" stimulates Marjorie Perloff to the shrewd observation that Merwin's deeper style is conservative in its rhetoric.

Jarold Ramsey touchingly notes in "The River of Bees" Merwin's eloquent quest for identity; while Cary Nelson helpfully studies echoes of political squalors in "The Asians Dying," which cause the poem's images to decay even as they associate. "Departure's Girl-Friend," a perpetually astonishing poem, is seen by Edward J. Brunner as another of Merwin's breakthroughs into what Emerson called "the Newness."

INTRODUCTION
Harold Bloom

> I mean we have yet no man who has leaned entirely on his
> character, and eaten angels' food; who, trusting to his
> sentiments, found life made of miracles; who, working for
> universal aims, found himself fed, he knew not how;
> clothed, sheltered, and weaponed, he knew not how, and
> yet it was done by his own hands.
> —EMERSON, *The Transcendentalist* (1842)

My subject is a still little-noted phenomenon, the revival of the
Native Strain or Emersonian vision, in the poetry of my own
generation of American poets, born in the decade 1925–1935. I
cannot survey all these poets here, and will discuss aspects of the
work of only three: W.S. Merwin, A.R. Ammons, and John
Ashbery. My choice is affected by the limitations of personal
taste, and I know it could be argued that the true continuators of
the Emersonian strain are to be located elsewhere, not so much
in the School of Stevens and Frost as in that of Williams and
Pound. But I am troubled by the equivocal nature (as it seems to
me) of the achievement of Olson, Duncan and their fellows,
down to Ginsberg, Snyder and younger figures. Emersonian
poetry is a diffuse though recognizable tradition: it includes
Jeffers as well as Hart Crane, the Pound of *The Pisan Cantos*
together with the Stevens of "The Auroras of Autumn," middle
Roethke just as much as the later Aiken. The problem of
American poetry after Emerson might be defined as: "Is it
possible to be un-Emersonian, rather than, at best, anti-
Emersonian?" Poe is not an Emersonian poet, but then he is also
not a good poet. Perhaps only our Southern poets, down to Tate
and Warren, could be as un-Emersonian as they were anti-
Emersonian; the best of them now (Dickey and Ammons) are
wholly Emersonian. Even in Emerson's own time, irreconcilable
poets emerged from his maelstrom: Dickinson, Thoreau,
Whitman, Very, even Tuckerman, whom Winters judged to be as

firm a reaction against Emerson as Hawthorne and Melville were. American Romanticism is larger than Emersonianism, but in our time it may no longer be possible to distinguish between the two phenomena. The prophet of a national poetic sensibility in America was the Concord rhapsode, who contains in the dialectical mysteries of his doctrines and temperament very nearly everything that has come after.

Let me begin with a representative text, by the indubitably representative poet of my generation, the Protean Merwin. The poem is the wonderful "The Way to the River" from the volume, *The Moving Target*, of 1963. As the poem is about fifty lines, I will summarize rather than quote it entire. Addressed to the poet's wife, the poem is a kind of middle-of-the-journey declaration, a creedal hymn reaffirming a covenant of love and a sense of poetic vocation. Historically (and prophetically) the poem sums up the dilemma of "the Silent Generation" of young Americans, on the eve of the astonishing change (or collapse) of sensibility that was to begin at Berkeley in 1964. After nearly a decade, one sees how brief an episode (or epicycle) this Time of Troubles was. Merwin, with his curious proleptic urgency, memorably caught the prelude to that time:

The way to the river leads past the names of
Ash the sleeves the wreaths of hinges
Through the song of the bandage vendor

I lay your name by my voice
As I go
The way to the river leads past the late
Doors and the games of the children born
*   looking backwards*
They play that they are broken glass
The numbers wait in the halls and the clouds
Call
From windows
They play that they are old they are putting the
*   horizon*

Into baskets they are escaping they are
Hiding

I step over the sleepers the fires the calendars
My voice turns to you

This is the "poverty" of Emerson and Stevens: imaginative need. Merwin joins a tradition that includes the E. A. Robinson of "The Man Against the Sky," the Frost of "Directive," the Stevens of "The Auroras of Autumn" as he too follows Emerson in building an altar to the Beautiful Necessity:

To the city of wines I have brought home a
    handful
Of water I walk slowly
In front of me they are building the empty
Ages I see them reflected not for long
Be here I am no longer ashamed of time it is too
    brief its hands
Have no names
I have passed it I know

Oh Necessity you with the face you with
All the faces

This is written on the back of everything

But we
Will read it together

The Merwin of this—still his present phase—began with the central poem, "Lemuel's Blessing," which follows the Smart of "Jubilate Agno" for its form (as do so many recent American poets, including Ginsberg, Strand, Donald Finkel) but which is also an Emersonian manifesto. Addressing a Spirit ("You that know the way") Merwin prayed: "Let the memory of tongues not unnerve me so that I stumble or quake." This hymn to Self-

Reliance expanded into the most ambitious poem of *The Moving Target*, a majestic celebration of what Emerson called the Newness, "For Now:" "Goodbye what you learned for me I have to learn anyway / You that forgot your rivers they are gone / Myself I would not know you." In *The Lice*, his next volume (and his best), Merwin defined the gods as "what has failed to become of us," a dark postscript to the Emersonian insistence that the poets are as liberating gods. The poems of *The Lice* are afflicted by light, as in this wholly characteristic brief lyric, the poignant "How We Are Spared":

> *At midsummer before dawn an orange light*
> *   returns to the mountains*
> *Like a great weight and the small birds cry out*
> *And bear it up*

With his largest volume, *The Carrier of Ladders*, Merwin appears to have completed his metamorphosis into an American visionary poet. The book's most astonishing yet most problematic poems are four ode-like "Psalms," subtitled: "Our Fathers," "The Signals," "The September Vision" and "The Cerements." No recent American poet, not even the Roethke of *The Far Field* or Dickey in his latest work has attempted so exalted a style:

> *I am the son of hazard but does my prayer*
> *   reach you O star of the uncertain*
> *I am the son of blindness but nothing that we*
> *   have made watches us*
> *I am the son of untruth but I have seen the*
> *   children in Paradise walking in pairs each*
> *   hand in hand with himself*
> *I am the son of the warder but he was buried*
> *   with his keys*
> *I am the son of the light but does it call me*
> *   Samuel or Jonah*
> *I am the son of a wish older than water but I*
> *   needed till now*

> *I am the son of ghosts clutching the world like*
> *roads but tomorrow I will go a new way*

The form is again that of the "Jubilate Agno," but the most important line in this first "Psalm," and in all of Merwin, is very far from Smart's pious spirit:

> *I am the son of the future but my own father*

As a poet, this latest Merwin hardly approaches that impossible self-begetting; the accent of the Pound-Eliot tradition hovers everywhere in even the most self-consciously bare of these verses. Merwin is more impressive for his terrible need, his lust for discontinuity, than for any actual inventiveness. The poignance of his current phase is the constant attempt at self-reliance, in the conviction that only thus will the poet see. Merwin's true precursors are three honorable, civilized representative poets: Longfellow and MacLeish and Wilbur, none of whom attempted to speak a Word that was his own Word only. In another time, Merwin would have gone on with the cultivation of a more continuous idiom, as he did in his early volumes, and as Longfellow did even in the Age of Emerson. The pressures of the quasi-apocalyptic nineteen-sixties have made of Merwin an American Orphic bard despite the sorrow that his poetic temperament is not at home in suffering the Native Strain. No poet legitimately speaks a Word whose burden is that his generation will be the very last. Merwin's litanies of denudation will read very oddly when a fresh generation proclaims nearly the same dilemma, and then yet another generation trumpets finality.

Merwin's predicament (and I hope I read it fairly, as I am not unsympathetic to his work) is that he has no Transcendental vision, and yet feels impelled to prophesy. What is fascinating is that after one hundred and thirty years, the situation of American poetry is precisely as it was when Emerson wrote his loving but ironic essay on his younger contemporaries and followers, *The Transcendentalist*, where they are seen as exposing our poverty but also their own. With that genial desperation (or desperate geniality) that is so endearing (and enraging) a quality in his work, Emerson nevertheless urged his followers out into the wilderness:

> But all these of whom I speak are not proficients; they are novices; they only show the road in which man should travel, when the soul has greater health and prowess. Yet let them feel the dignity of their charge, and deserve a larger power. Their heart is the ark in which the fire is concealed which shall burn in a broader and universal flame. Let them obey the Genius then most when his impulse is wildest; then most when he seems to lead to uninhabitable deserts of thought and life; for the path which the hero travels alone is the highway of health and benefit to mankind. What is the privilege and nobility of our nature but its persistency, through its power to attach itself to what is permanent?

Merwin prays to be sustained during his time in the desert, but his poems hardly persuade us that his Genius or Spirit has led him into "uninhabitable deserts of thought and life." Readers distrustful of *The Carrier of Ladders* either emphasize what they feel is a dominance of style over substance or they complain of spiritual pretentiousness. What I find more problematic is something that Emerson foresaw when he said of his Transcendentalist that "He believes in miracle, in the perpetual openness of the human mind to new influx of light and power; he believes in inspiration, and in ecstasy," and went on to observe that such a youth was part of an American literature and spiritual history still "in the optative mood." Merwin's optative mood seems only to concern his impersonal identity as poet-prophet; instead of a belief in an influx of light and power, he offers us what we might contrive to know anyway, even if we had not been chilled with him by his artful mutations:

> *To which I make my way eating the silence of*
>   *animals*
> *Offering snow to the darkness*
>
> *Today belongs to few and tomorrow to no one*

Emerson's favorite oracular guise was as an Orphic poet. Of the Orphic deities—Eros, Dionysus, and Ananke—Merwin gives us some backward glances at the first, and a constant view of the last, but the Dionysiac has gone out of his poetry. Without the Bacchic turbulence, and haunted by a light that he presents as wholly meaningless, Merwin seems condemned to write a poetry that is as bare of true content as it is so elegantly bare in diction and design. Only the *situation* of the Emersonian Transcendentalist or Orphic Poet survives in Merwin; it is as though for him the native strain were pure strain, to be endured because endurance is value enough, or even because the eloquence of endurance is enough.

W.S. Merwin

The son of a Presbyterian minister, William Stanley Merwin was born on September 30, 1927, in New York City but was raised in Union City, New Jersey, an industrial town just outside of New York. He later lived in Scranton, Pennsylvania, at the time a thriving steel and industrial city. Merwin began writing at a very young age. Jay Parini, in Ian Hamilton's *Oxford Companion to Twentieth-Century Poetry in English*, quoted Merwin as saying, "I started writing hymns for my father as soon as I could write at all." The formality of hymns, as well as the individual spiritualism of the forms, is a fit prelude to what his poetry would evolve into, during its three distinct phases.

Merwin attended Princeton University and studied with John Berryman and R. P. Blackmur. He has told interviewers that he was not the model student; he spent much time walking and hanging out near the horse stables, and often did not pay any attention to what happened in class. Reportedly, Blackmur, Berryman, and Herman Broch were more useful to Merwin as mentors. In a long quotation in a interview with Gale Publishing's *Contemporary Authors*, Merwin characterized the three men as teaching "by example as much as by design."

He graduated Princeton and, after an extra year of graduate study in languages, Merwin began traveling through Europe. He mostly visited England, France, and Spain, and for a short time was a tutor to Portugal's royal family. By 1950, he accepted a position as a private tutor to the son of Robert Graves, the poet and novelist, author of *I Claudius*. While the post only lasted for one year, some have speculated that Merwin gained his appreciation for mythology from Graves, himself an authority on various mythologies, particularly Greek.

In 1951, Merwin moved to London, where he found work translating Spanish and French literary classics for broadcast by the British Broadcasting Company. His translation work there established a reputation sufficient for him to continue to find translation work in the decades that followed. Ever since, Merwin has been just as prolific a translator as he has been a poet, winning many awards for his work throughout his career.

But his time abroad did not come without complication. Merwin has said that his time in England, in particular, left him "discontented." His feeling of alienation from America led him to consider what the mythological and actual aspects of America were; such concerns have caused critic Ed Folsom and some others to examine parallels between Whitman and Merwin. Merwin said that those considerations led to the specific, seemingly confessional lyrics of *The Drunk in the Furnace*, but also to later, more abstract, paradoxical and mythological thinking about our cultural and natural landscapes.

Merwin's career as a poet received an enormous boost when, in 1952, W.H. Auden selected *A Mask for Janus* as the winner of the Yale Younger Poets prize, one of the most prestigious awards in American poetry. Auden proclaimed Merwin a technical master, and *A Mask for Janus* was a complex, lush example of formal poetry, full of the potential that Merwin would unlock in the decades to come. Critics have praised the volume's awareness of line, noted its mythological subject matter, and pointed at its ornate language as a paradoxical gift that Merwin would rebel against in his later work. Because of the radical difference between Merwin's work at the beginning of his career and his most recent work, critic and poet David Mason has described Merwin as "our most protean poet."

In the 1960s, Merwin began to develop and change his style forcefully, as some of the excerpts and analyses which follow will discuss. Initially, the abrupt departure was dismissed by a number of critics. Richard Howard points out, however, that James Dickey saw the direction of the poet's work, and rightly noted the roots of Merwin's radical departure in the volumes which preceded it. His most enduring volumes have come from that period: *The Drunk in the Furnace, The Lice, The Carrier of Ladders*, and *The Moving Target*. In 1970, *The Carrier of Ladders* earned Merwin the Pulitzer Prize. He has gone on to win the Bollingen Prize, in 1979, two Guggenheim Fellowships, *Poetry* magazine's

Lenore Marshall Prize, and a Lila Wallace/Reader's Digest fellowship.

Merwin has never held a teaching position at a university, which is rare among his contemporaries. The early success of his books, coupled with his ability to make money translating, has meant that he has supported himself professionally as a writer, and never as a teacher. He is twice divorced, and lives with his current wife, Paula Schwartz. He currently resides in Hawaii, where he has lived since the late 1970s, and where he is in the process of reclaiming an old pineapple plantation, attempting to restore to the spot the native species which comprised it and made it a rainforest. He continues to publish poetry in leading periodicals in the United States and Great Britain, and is considered one of our greatest living poets.

A NOTE ON THE TEXT:

Quoting Merwin provides some editorial difficulties for those trying to observe traditional grammatical rules in English. Because Merwin's later work eschews standard punctuation marks for the variety of artistic effects it affords, one has to make decisions on how to present short quotations without affecting the line meaning through the insertion of punctuation. If one, for instance, ends a sentence with a quote, it may not be clear whether the period is Merwin's or the critic's, since convention is to place the period within the quotation marks. Thus, I have tried to be consistent in breaking the rule which places commas, periods, question marks, and the like within quotation marks. When quoting Merwin, I place all of my punctuation marks *outside* the quotation marks in order that it is clear to every reader that the punctuation is indeed mine, for clarity, and not Merwin's. Should any punctuation appear *within* quotation marks, it can be assumed that Merwin wanted it there.

CRITICAL ANALYSIS OF
"The Drunk in the Furnace"

While one of Merwin's most famous poems, it is very different from the overwhelming majority of the poet's work. It typifies the lush, erudite, formal approaches of his first four books, and especially captures the religious themes so present in eponymous collection. However, many critics, including ones excerpted in this volume, have remarked that the poem represents the apex of Merwin's early approach, and an important piece to transition him from a mode of narrative lyricism to one more spare, more mythological, and more universal.

The formal structure of the poem is visible at once. The seven line stanzas each begin and end with short, three-stress lines. Between the lines bracketing each stanzas, five lines of five stresses each fill the stanzas. In their shape on the page, the stanzas even suggest furnaces, with their pipe-top short lines and their squat, full middles. The form, however, is parody, with roots in rhyme royal, another seven-line stanza pattern typical of medieval and early modern poetry, a style similar to other elaborate patterns employed by the poet in his first collections.

Throughout the poem, however, Merwin undermines poetic tradition, religion, society, and more, in a burlesque display of perversity. The opening line, "For a good decade" can be read two ways: as the plain-spoken approximation of time, or as a statement giving the decade a value, "good". The word's contrast to what follows is marked and intentional.

During the decade, the furnace "stood in the naked gulley, fireless"—or, under-employed, useless, a thing no longer used rightly. In some ways, too, if one considers the masculine figure of the drunk, the furnace is emasculated, "fireless", as incapable and, perhaps, unholy, as the drunk himself. Given the subtext of religion in the poem (to be discussed further below), a fireless furnace is somewhat akin to a toothless hell, a punishment of little consequence. It is here where the drunk will reside.

But, for the opening of the poem, it is also "vacant as any hat", a mildly absurd statement on the face of it, but an absurdity that makes intuitive sense insomuch as a hat, without a head, is vacant. The comparison of emptiness to a piece of clothing unworn is a typical image for Merwin, and one made more significant with advent of the drunk, and the reader's understanding that a hat found near a decrepit furnace would be something the drunk would wear.

The images continue to imply decrepitude, age, and hugeness: the furnace is a "hulking black fossil" that would "erode unnoticed with the rest of the junk hill/ by the poisonous creek" until it, too, was something else piled on their "ignorance". The sounds repeated in that first stanza, the hard 'k' and the slurry 'l' and 's,' contribute to the sense of dismissal and corruption Merwin is cultivating, laying ground for the perversion of the poem's end.

In the second stanza, the drunk appears, fulfilling the foreshadowing and embodying the tone of the first stanza. "They were afterwards astonished" at seeing him. The "they" is an abstraction typical of the kind Merwin will make in his subsequent work, but in the context of this poem it also does the duty of standing in for a number of people. It can refer to the upstanding community members, the Reverend's close followers, or the "witless offspring" of the end. "They" are all astonished for different reasons, as the poem lets readers now.

They "confirm, one morning, a twist of smoke", an image calling to mind the Papal selection techniques in Rome but, more pressingly, the presence, perhaps *threatening* presence, of something alive. In this case, it is a person alive in a place thought to harbor nothing, to give nothing, a wasteland of sorts. That they "confirm" his presence is also important, because the many meanings of confirm include the religious one, to induct an individual into the faith with a solemn pledge of belief. The existence of the drunk is also something of a leap of faith; he is not, at any point in the poem, present aside from signs that he is present: the smoke, the sound of bed springs, the "Hammer-and-anvilling" from inside the furnace. There is no way to "confirm" his existence other than through the signs of his disturbance of the otherwise quiet, "naked gulley".

The smoke itself, beyond the Papal associations, is "like a pale/ Resurrection," so that the existence of life in the furnace is dramatically compared with the ascension of Christ. That Christ ascends from a furnace, a hell, is a sacrilege, just as the drunk's presence near so reverent a body of people is, to them, a sacrilege. The drunk, whose damaged presence is dressed in holy imagery, is a reciprocal of Christ, or antichrist. The drunk so corrupts his environs that the smoke itself is "staggering out of its chewed hole," an image at once inebriate and used up.

But Merwin's tone treats the drunk such that readers do not feel the same menace that Merwin implies in his word choices. The poem rhymes, has a four-beat dance to its lines, with three-stress lead-ins and outros, such that it resembles a song as well as a formal, more courtly poem. Such light treatment juxtaposed with the subject matter suggests the speaker's attitude is less pious than the congregation referred to in the poem's later stanzas.

After spotting the smoke, the observers also "remark" on "other tokens" that the drunk, identified only as "someone," has left as evidence that within the furnace he had "established/ His bad castle." The stanza has yet more juxtaposition: "cosily bolted", "eye-holed iron", and "drafty burner" all testify to the mixed messages the onlookers take in while looking at the "bad castle." "Bad castle" especially captures the oxymoron of the drunk; his dereliction is huge, as befits a castle, but it is a castle of rot, of emptiness, and so, "bad". But as the juxtaposition builds, and Merwin effectively describes a failed man in royal and religious turns, the celebration of imperfection develops, becoming the message from which the offspring will learn.

In the first sentence of the next stanza ("Where he gets his spirits/ It's a mystery."), the conspicuous line break plays with the meaning of spirits, again contrasting the holy meaning of the word with its terrestrial meaning as a euphemism for drink. The line could be read to mean that it's unclear how he comes by his constitution or by his booze. The fact that no one sees him get the booze, despite the attraction of his lair to the local youth, casts some doubt on whether the affliction that has him living in a furnace is really booze at all. In the next lines, however, it is clear that *something* makes him behave oddly.

> The stuff keeps him musical:
> Hammer-and-anvilling with poker and bottle
> To his jugged bellowings, till the last groaning clang
> As he collapses onto the rioting
> Springs of a litter of car seats ranged on the grates,
>   To sleep like an iron pig.

He is, of course, singing and clanging about drunkenly, and again Merwin's sonic play imitates the sound that would be emanating from the furnace. Again, the imagery of the fire and the forge is at work, with the poker, the bellowings, the anvil. Even the last line of the stanza contains an inversion important to anyone who grew up in steel country. Pig iron is unrefined iron taken from a blast furnace prior to working it into steel or other alloys. The inversion preserves the sense of being unrefined, while characterizing his piggish habits as hardened into something like iron.

The hardened nature of the trunk is contrasted against the flimsy "tar-paper" church of the next stanza, where the Reverend is hammering home a point of scripture that deals with hell as a furnace, with "stoke-holes that are sated never". In other words, the furnace cannot ever have enough. The Reverend's implication is that Hell will never be exhausted by an abundance of fuel; it can handle all the sinners and more. The text is a warning, delivered by a man lingering over a book rather than presiding over the ruin outside his church. The congregation, convinced they are in a site of hallowed ground, "nod and hate trespassers." The meaning of trespasses is another Merwin double, meaning both those who are squatters (living in unapproved structures, like furnaces, on property not their own) as well as those who act against the word of God, or sinners.

At this point, the poem swings on a hinge that brings the reader back, out of the church, to the furnace:

> When the furnace wakes, though, all afternoon
> Their witless offspring flock like piped rats to its siren

> Crescendo, and agape on the crumbling ridge
>   Stand in a row and learn.

The enjambment at "afternoon" lends the line some ambiguity of meaning—either that the furnace is in a constant waking, or that the offspring stand there all day. They come like piped rats, an allusion to the Pied Piper of Hamlein, who lured rats from the town and to their death. As well, that the furnace is a "siren" refers to the mythological creatures who attempted to lure Odysseus to his death during his voyage to return home. By comparing the children to rats, and the drunk to a siren, the speaker of the poem spares none of the people within from a removed scorn. Even in the last lines, it is unabated, if complicated. The siren is a "crescendo," the peak of frenzy, something precipitating a calm, afterward. Their calm comes in what they see, standing on the ridge, "agape". Once again, the word choice is particular and layered. Agape can mean stunned, but it derives that meaning from an earlier, Greek meaning, Agape, or love of God. They are both stunned and worshipful. And of what—the drunk, or the furnace, as the furnace is the subject of those final four lines?

The contradictions of what the offspring are worshipping in the furnace seem little more comforting than the austerities offered by the Reverend who, it should be noted, is described only in terms of his congregation, who "hate". The menace of the two options—the earthly and the humanly-derived idea of the heavenly—is typical of the warning tone and the obsession with death that would come later in Merwin's work. As well, because the hell of the furnace is fireless, it is also harmless, and not intimidating. The "witless offspring" do not, then, witness any Calvinistic fate for the drunk. They see someone broken, terrible, horrific, but ultimately of no consequence on earth nor in heaven. They learn a legacy of death and meaninglessness.

CRITICAL VIEWS ON
"The Drunk in the Furnace"

RICHARD HOWARD ON THE POEM'S CHAOS

[Richard Howard is the author of eleven volumes of poetry, including *Untitled Subjects*, for which he received the Pulitzer Prize. He has published more than 150 translations from the French, as well, including Baudelaire's *Les Fleurs du mal*, for which he received the 1983 American Book Award for translation. He is also the author of *Alone with America: Essays on the Art of Poetry in the United States since 1950*, first published in 1969 and expanded in 1980. He was Poet Laureate of New York State (1994–96) and is currently the poetry editor of *The Paris Review* and *Western Humanities Review*. He teaches in the Writing Division of the School of the Arts, Columbia University. In this piece, excerpted from a longer essay on Merwin (the longest piece, in fact, in the entirety of *Alone with America*), Howard comments on the ways in which the chaos in the poem represents an emerging strength and battle in the poet's work.]

It is interesting to note contemporary reactions to this book, the comment being neatly divided between regret for the surrendered "techniques of one of the master prosodists of our time" and, as James Dickey (whose qualification of Merwin's new diction as "roughed-up, clunking" I have already cited) put it, "an impression that this poet, though he may now seem to be stalled after a prodigal beginning, is gathering force." Observing with characteristic asperity that Merwin was now past "the intricacies of what is so easy for him to say concerning almost anything," Dickey predicted—and he was the only critic at this stage who saw his way so far into Merwin's intentions, so violently realized in the subsequent volumes—that "he should soar like a phoenix out of the neat ashes of his early work." The image of the phoenix, a creature which repeatedly consumes itself in order to reappear altogether different though still ... the phoenix, jibes precisely with the disquieting but authentic succession of accomplishments we confront in Merwin today.

The fourth book closes, significantly, with its title poem, "The Drunk in the Furnace," which we must consider as a fulfillment of the epigraph to *The Dancing Bears*, to wit, Flaubert's bitter observation that our speech is as the hammering on a cracked kettle to make bears dance, when we would seduce the stars—in order to record Merwin's advance—or is it a retreat?—to his own chaos from a borrowed or inherited order. The poem sets one of his typically graceless scenes: the deprived community ("in their tar-paper church ... they nod and hate trespassers") and, in the naked gully out back, a huge scrapped furnace:

> *No more to them than a hulking black fossil*
> *To erode unnoticed with the rest of the junk-hill*
> *By the poisonous creek, and rapidly to be added*
>   *To their ignorance—*

An unaccountable drunk ("where he gets his spirits / it's a mystery") takes up residence inside, to the scandal of these bigots, and there performs his preposterous rites:

> *Hammer-and-anvilling with poker and bottle*
> *To his jugged bellowings, till the last groaning clang*
> *As he collapses ...*

But though the booze-ridden minstrel is deplored in "his bad castle," the smoke is said to stagger out of its "chewed hole like a pale resurrection," and when the furnace-music wakes,

>   *... all afternoon*
> *Their witless offspring flock like piped rats to its siren*
> *Crescendo, and agape on the crumbling ridge*
>   *Stand in a row and learn.*

This is the apotheosis of Merwin's emblem of the poet, his progress-report, this comic horror which for all its obloquy and abuse is yet redeemed by the consistency and energy, by the reality of the treatment. It is one quality of an important writer that the exigencies of his form—whether they be the celebrations of an order or the "jugged bellowings" of a chaos—become not the flaws of his work but its strength, and in each phase of Merwin's accomplishment, we can observe the same extremity of commitment and the same phoenix-like consummation. Here, certainly, the ashes are not the least bit neat, but rather the desperate calcination of a man in a death-struggle (what else could it be?) with his own *realization*, in all the senses that word will bear, of mortality.

—Richard Howard, *Alone with America: Essays on the Art of Poetry in the United States since 1950* (New York: Atheneum, 1980): pp. 433–434.

CHERI DAVIS ON THE POEM AS MERWIN'S METAPHORICAL HOME

[Cheryl Davis Langdell (Cheri Davis) is Associate Professor of modern languages and literature at California Baptist University. She is the author of *W. S. Merwin* as well as numerous articles on the poet. In the excerpt, Davis describes the poem as Merwin's "poetic residence."]

Having distinguished himself from the descendants, Merwin chooses for his poetic residence "the real dark" of the unknown, the mystery of life. He sums up the enigma of the known in this comment: "Daily the indispensable is taught to elude us, while we are furnished according to our wishes with armories of what we do not need" (H, 94). What he needs exists in the blind depths, the uncharted reaches to which he retreats from myth (Olympus and Minerva), the Protestant God, and other conventions imposed on him by civilized society. In the title poem of the book Merwin envisions how he might better explore the perimeters of the mysterious:

> For a good decade
> The furnace stood in the naked gully, fireless
> And vacant as any hat. Then when it was
> No more to them than a hulking black fossil
> To erode unnoticed with the rest of the junk-hill
> By the poisonous creek, and rapidly to be added
> To their ignorance,
> They were afterwards astonished
> To confirm, one morning, a twist of smoke like a pale
> Resurrection. (F, 261)

Merwin's conventional early style is "a hulking black fossil," "vacant as any hat." He does not personally inhabit any of the earlier poems. In fact, they are so objective, so mythic as to be anonymous. Although in 1960, he feels he has earned the reputation of a poet of stature, he knows if he persists in the exquisitely impersonal early style, he will rapidly be consigned to oblivion. He, like his ancestors, will be a relic of the past, rapidly be "added" to the sum of the world's "ignorance." His personal poetic voice is only here emerging in the guise of a "twist of smoke like a pale / Resurrection." This new life is "confirmed" by onlookers, the natives' "witless offspring" and critics. They begin to

> ... remark then other tokens that someone
> Cosily bolted behind the eye-holed iron
> Door of the drafty burner, had there established
> His bad castle.
> Where he gets his spirits
> It's a mystery. But the stuff keeps him musical!
> Hammer-and-anvilling with poker and bottle
> To his jugged bellowings, till the last groaning clang
> As he collapses onto the rioting
> Springs of a litter of car-seats ranged on the grates,
> To sleep like an iron pig. (F, 261)

Richard Howard considers "The Drunk in the Furnace" "a fulfillment of the epigraph to *The Dancing Bears*, to wit, Flaubert's bitter observation that our speech is as the hammering on a cracked kettle to make bears dance, when we would seduce the stars." He sees it as a recording of "Merwin's advance—or is it a retreat?—to his own chaos from a borrowed or inherited order."[14] The order Merwin here establishes for himself within the furnace is a domain where he makes "religious, almost sacred noises with his bottle" and poker.[15] He then passes into an alcoholic stupor and silence. The drunk sleeps in "His bad castle" "like an iron pig." "Where he gets his spirits / It's a mystery." But the poem, like the drunk and Merwin's voice, is redeemed by vitality and consistency.[16] "The Drunk in the Furnace" concludes:

> In their tar-paper church
> On a text about stoke-holes that are sated never
> Their reverend lingers. They nod and hate trespassers.
> When the furnace wakes, though, all afternoon
> Their witless offspring flock like piped rats to its siren
> Crescendo, and agape on the crumbling ridge
> Stand in a row and learn. (F, 261)

An immovable barrier is set up between poet and hearer. Henceforth the poet will preach in "his juggled bellowing" on a "text about stoke-holes"; the readers will "Stand in a row and learn." "The outside world is in awe of the drunk and learns as much from his silence as from his noise."[17] The welling, provident flow of his "music" is the central focus, the only possible focus, of interest; it is the creative justification of the drunk/poet's existence. "It is at this point that Merwin decided that he no longer wishes merely to locate and observe the abyss; he wants to explore it; he wants to become the drunk in the furnace. The furnace, of course, is himself, his body and his inner life. To do this he knows that his way of speaking must change. His poems must not merely notice silence, they must to the extent possible, become silence. At least they must be made of both the drunk's sacred thumping and stupor."

Like the drunk in the furnace, Merwin sits in the darkness composing a poetry of absence, silence, and the clanging words that emerge from his own chaos. It is a poetry comprised in part of "images of what I never had." "It has taken me this long to learn what I cannot say / where it begins like the names of the hungry" (CL, 28). His rolling crescendos will display the mind in the process of finding meaning within the furnace, finding words and spaces that will suffice to account for his experience of it. He has been resurrected from the family "junk-hill," saved from "ignorance," so off and on he will continue playing in the furnace even as the established orders of society, morality, poetry, and religion are crumbling like sinking ships. The assonance of "bad castle" signals the drunk's felicitous discovery of a cosy home and hearth. He may remain here, educating the offspring in the inward way of truth, teaching the innocent their "bad" catechism. Having found this new residence, he proclaims it as the home he will from time to time return to. In his next book, *The Moving Target*, published three years later, some poems come from within the furnace while some merely point out the scope of mystery and silence, "the terror which cannot be charted." If in the new book his aim is unsteady, after all a moving target is harder to hit.

NOTES

14. *Alone With America*, pp. 370–71.
15. "Speaking from Within the Furnace," p. 4.
16. *Alone With America*, p. 371.
17. All quotations in this paragraph from "Speaking from Within the Furnace," p. 4.

—Cheri Davis, *W. S. Merwin* (Boston: Twayne Publishers, 1981): pp. 72–75.

CARY NELSON ON MERWIN'S REPUDIATION OF EARLY STYLE

[Cary Nelson is Jubilee Professor of Liberal Arts and Sciences at the University of Illinois at Urbana-Champaign. He is the editor and author of numerous books, including *Manifesto of a*

Tenured Radical, the *Oxford Anthology of Modern American Poetry, Repression and Recovery: Modern American Poetry and the Politics of Cultural Memory, 1910–1945,* and *Revolutionary Memory: Recovering the Poetry of the American Left.* He has also published several volumes on the Spanish Civil War, including a collection of letters. In this excerpt, Nelson shows how Merwin's "burlesque of all his own overwrought rhetoric" signals a stylistic departure in his work.]

Two poems are especially relevant to Merwin's next book. In "Sailor Ashore" a drunk's vision reveals ironically "what unsteady ways the solid earth has / After all" (*DF,* 7). There follows, masked with buffoonery, the kind of unnerving perception so frequent in Merwin's work since *The Moving Target*: "the sea is everywhere. / But worst here where it is secret and pretends / To keep its mountains in one place." The drunk's classic perception of the animacy of inanimate objects and forces anticipates what will become one of Merwin's characteristic syntactic and semantic devices.

The final poem in the book, which is also the title poem, is an irrevocable perspective on his work to that point. An empty iron furnace rusts in a trash-ridden gully by a poisonous creek, until a derelict decides to make it his "bad castle." He brings his bottle, bolts the door behind him, and carouses in drunken solitude until he passes out. Written in careful septets, the poem's formal concern for a frivolous occasion mocks all the sonorities of Merwin's previous books. The poem ends with a description of the local adults listening to warnings from their preacher, while their children crowd to the irresistible furnace:

> Their witless offspring flock like piped rats to its siren
> Crescendo, and agape on the crumbling ridge
>   Stand in a row and learn.
>
>   (*DF,* 54)

With this burlesque of all his own overwrought rhetoric, Merwin can never return to his earlier style. It is a deliberate aggression.

This rebirth of willful failure is a singularly American trait. It is common to many of our foremost poets, and crucial to many ruined or limited careers whose poetry nevertheless holds us. Of the several hundred poems Merwin has published since 1960, many do not succeed; some, like the run-on Beckettian sentence of "Fear" (*CL*, 83–86), are simply not appropriate to his new form. A few, like "Line" (*CF*, 26), which describes the ritual interactions in a supermarket line, deal with prosaic topics that resist Merwin's powers of transformation and thus become comic, a tendency he finally masters in "Questions to Tourists Stopped by a Pineapple Field" (*OH*, 43–45). Some, like many of his short prose pieces, seem glibly designed to indulge a lazy audience's pleasure in effortless and unspecific mystery. Others demand too much of themselves and of their readers, as when Merwin-like Rich in "Not Somewhere Else, But Here" in *The Dream of a Common Language* and Duncan in "The Fire" in *Bending The Bow*—tries to render a series of unconnected images into a condition of heightened apprehension: "an end a wise man fire / other stars the left hand" (*WA*, 101). Many, such as the haiku-like fragments in "Signs" (*CL*, 116–18), pale before the overwhelming power of his best work. Yet the production, like Whitman's work, is a single enterprise; the volumes beginning with *The Moving Target* are all one book, even to the ultimate undermining of the project in the optimistic poems in *The Compass Flower* and *Finding the Islands*. The poems reflect one another endlessly, repeat the same messages tirelessly, clarify one another and simultaneously complicate one another until no image can ever be resolved.

It is not merely that we must judge the body of poems entire. It is rather, as with Rich, that the finest poems are always in dialogue with the worst. Though new subjects are frequently introduced, many of the major poems use a vocabulary (silence, emptiness, distance, darkness, whiteness, death) and create images with nouns (gloves, hands, eyes, feet, shoes, water, birds, mirrors, sky, trees, nests, wings) whose familiarity surpasses a verbal signature and becomes almost a form of self-betrayal. What we experience in the best poems is a cohesion *despite* this omnipresent diction. The best wrest themselves from their rhetorical ground and make themselves simultaneously unique and typical. Merwin exploits the most impossible fact of language—that words and images are riddled with received meaning and historical context. Like Kenneth Burke, Merwin believes that language is not merely a web of connotations but also a structured source of motivation. Unlike Burke and Duncan, however, Merwin does not feel that play amidst these verbal connections will be liberating. Language is already a democratic resource, but it is suffocating. Our words speak through us to override any fresh use we may have for them. "On the way to them," he writes, "the words / Die" (*L*, 7); they are used, given, and they will not live for us. "I can put my words into the mouths / of spirits," he tells us, "but they will not say them" (*CL*, 17).

Merwin is not the first to have wrestled in this way with poetic tradition; indeed, his first books are damaged by influences never made truly his own. Merwin is, however, unique in so daringly disclosing the echolalic qualities of his own language. Beckett and Burroughs, along with many younger novelists, have taken that risk in prose, but our preconceptions about the formal integrity of poems make the choice more difficult there. Because of those expectations, the ironic formal repetition and verbal self-subversion so common in experimental fiction have yet to be attempted with much success in contemporary poetry.[5] The most radical other example is James Merrill, with the plural, unstable texture he achieves by juxtaposing original metaphors, conversational clichés, and frequent allusion and quotation. It is not surprising that neither Merwin's nor Merrill's very different kinds of self-deflating irony have been successfully imitated, since most open-form contemporary American poetry retains some Whitmanesque hope of projecting an ideally open and democratic society. Merwin's open forms, indeed, have succeeded in mirroring the loss of any real historical possibility. Unlike those poems of the 1960s that are grounded in a reaction against historical actuality, or even those poems that seem to be victimized by history, Merwin's poems manage to give our history its most frightening voice. The revolution in Merwin's style must, then, be understood as an exacting and necessary discipline, one which is highly responsive to the general political environment. (A specific example is his decision, two-thirds of the way through *The Moving Target* and again early in *The Lice*, to abandon all punctuation.)[6] This discipline is undertaken, somewhat like Beckett's decision to write in French, in the face of considerable self-doubt and a sensitivity to the supremely self-conscious state of language in this historical moment. He recognizes that poetry exhibits some of the most terrible and most transcendent dreams identified with American culture. "Is it with speech," he asks, that "you combed out your voice till the ends bled" (*L*, 39). "In / our language deaths are to be heard / at any moment through the talk" (*CL*, 56). To give voice to those deaths, as Eliot did in *The Waste Land* and as Merwin has succeeded in doing, is to become for a moment the single voice of an age.

NOTES

5. For an analysis of the relationship between Merwin's poetry and contemporary fiction, see Evan Watkins's *The Critical Act: Criticism and Community* (New Haven: Yale University Press, 1978).

6. Eliminating punctuation allows for some special effects that might be more self-conscious in a conventionally punctuated poem. Occasionally he will let the last line of a stanza bleed off into empty space: "but when she opened it" (*CL*, 126). Alternatively, he can limit that uncertainty with the following line, in this case the first line of the next stanza: "Someone has just / but no sound reaches the gate" (*CL*, 36). He will frequently embed a quotation within a line, without distinguishing punctuation, so that what would ordinarily be isolated seems instead to emerge inexorably from the preceding words: "I hear the cry go up for him Caesar Caesar" (*L*, 19); "I have prayed O wounds come back from death / and be healed" (*CL*, 96). See also Merwin's own comments on eliminating punctuation in his *Iowa Review* interview.

—Cary Nelson, "Merwin's Deconstructive Career." *W.S. Merwin: Essays on the Poetry*, Cary Nelson and Ed Folsom, eds. (Urbana: University of Illinois Press, 1987): pp. 88–91.

[Edward J. Brunner teaches in the English department at Southern Indiana University at Carbondale. He is the author of *Splendid Failure: Hart Crane and the Making of "The Bridge"* and *Poetry as Labor and Privilege: The Writings of W.S. Merwin* (University of Illinois Press, 1991). His most recent book, *Cold War Poetry*, reconsiders in detail the mainstream poetry of the 1950s. He is one of the Advisory Editors to the *Oxford Anthology of Modern American Poetry*. In the excerpt, Brunner argues that the style has the effect of positioning Merwin as an exile to the mainstream poetry community.]

Aggressively, self-consciously, defiantly, it reasserts themes in a new key chosen for its excruciating dissonance. The derelict who has "established / His bad castle" in an abandoned furnace never appears, but his residency can be deduced from "a twist of smoke" and "other tokens," and he becomes the subject of local sermons, though he draws the fascinated attention of the children who "flock like piped rats" as he bangs out a grotesque music of "Hammer-and-anvilling," "jugged bellowings," and "groaning clangs" bumping against the walls that confine him but that he will not leave. Mingling despair and anger, Merwin, like his derelict, refuses to go away, even as he realizes that he must go underground to survive—that the atmosphere is poison to him.[15]

The poem actively subvert's the pattern otherwise stamped on the family poems, that rigid division of interior and exterior. Being inside a furnace that has been discarded outside blurs any clear-cut distinction, and the poem poses two irreconcilable questions: Is the drunk's cloddishness all that the community deserves, his relegation to the edge of town revealing the narrowness of people who tidy up their environment by creating junkpiles at the edge of town for those they cannot comprehend? Or is the persistence of the drunk, minding his own business and making his harmless music as he wills, distilling his spirits into a clanking all his own, a lesson in individuality, in perseverance, through his recycling of what others would discard by reshaping it to an individual purpose that blithely ignores what others conventionally expect (as Merwin has managed to recycle the refuse of his family poems)? As these two irreconcilables clash, neither resolved, it is clear that Merwin has found a way, in anger and in anguish, to express his own reaction to being a poet in his own homeland. And yet who is the drunk in the furnace if not his grandfather, an invisible outsider, as Merwin the child knew him, consigned to his marginal role, innocent and oblivious of his stature as a rebel and iconoclast, an example for children to follow. The lesson they learn, quite different from the preacher's text on stoke-holes that are "sated never," is that one must leave this confined community, going further than the junkpile at the edge of town.

Often admired as a work that prophesied an impending change in Merwin's style, "The Drunk in the Furnace" establishes a complex vantage point from which Merwin can survey the wreckage of his family cycle. The poem is, like its central figure, both defiant and circumspect: it secretes stories, none of which are allowed to emerge. But in the context of the entire cycle, especially in the light of its reconstructed development, it is lucid enough. Merwin's homecoming revealed a ruined landscape inhabited by figures sullen, secretive, and withdrawn, and a cycle of poetry that had begun expansively hardened into an abrasive pattern. This unexpected turn ultimately led to a wider understanding of the America into which he had fallen. In the cycle as arranged for final publication, his homeland is the place in which the habit of forgetfulness has become thoroughly ingrained. What he understands is the fact of his own exclusion, and by the close he has found the only home available to him: the margins of the community, where he will dwell as an exile.

NOTE

15. Merwin's father, a minister, raged against the insatiable appetite of the coal-burning furnace in the family's Scranton home (*Unframed Originals*, pp. 179–84). Thus the poem also asks to be read as a family joke, and as a distorted

communication between Merwin and his father. Merwin's father used the costly furnace as an excuse to keep temperatures lower in selective parts of the house, in order to discourage a house guest of whom he disapproved and whom Merwin loved as a child.

—Edward J. Brunner, *Poetry as Labor and Privelege: The Writings of W.S. Merwin* (Urbana: University of Illinois Press, 1991): pp. 85–86.

H.L. HIX DISPUTES THE ROLE OF MERWIN'S FAMILY IN THE POEM

[H.L. Hix is vice president for academic affairs at the Cleveland Institute of Art. His most recent books are a poetry collection, *Surely As Birds Fly* (2002), and a collection of essays, *As Easy As Lying* (2000). His other books include *Rational Numbers* (2000), which won the T.S. Eliot Prize, and *Perfect Hell* (1996), which won the Peregrine Smith Poetry Award. He is also the author of critical books on W.S. Merwin and Willam H. Gass. Hix outlines the unlikeliness of familial roots for the characters in the poem.]

Calling "Grandfather in the Old Men's Home" a "very deliberate attempt to make a myth out of personal, private, and local material," Merwin explains that "my grandmother's generation was very fundamentalist Methodist and didn't believe in alcohol- I mean, there are those who believed that buttermilk was sinful because sometimes it had as much as two degrees in it.... My Grandfather was a pilot, so I'm told, on the Allegheny River and a legendary local drunk. And he was put into the old men's home by his sons."9 The myth he creates from that material tells of "the danger of embracing the constant and absolute rather than the conditional and ambiguous."10 His grandfather, who through life has tormented his grandmother by drunkenness, long absences, and dangerous unpredictability, has finally satisfied her: he is "gentle at last" (FF, 247). But she is too rigid, "wearing the true faith / Like an iron nightgown," and he pays a heavy price to satisfy her. "The fact that he can only attain such a condition through senility is a scathing attack on middle-class morality,"[11] and transforms this into a poem of departure, too, a vow not to become like "the children they both had begotten, / With old faces now, but themselves shrunken / To child-size again," who stood by their mother "Beating their little Bibles till he died."

The short-lived energy of the family poems in *The Drunk in the Furnace* prompts the departure in *The Moving Target*. "John Otto" and "Grandfather in the Old Men's Home" are expansive poems that move easily from a few facts to myth, but Edward J. Brunner points out that those poems were written while Merwin was in Europe. The poems he composed after his return to America, like "Grandmother Dying," contract to a much narrower scope, unable to escape the gravity of the facts,[12] with the result that his attack on the morality of those he portrays is no less scathing, but it is significantly less subtle. "Grandmother Dying" depicts a woman "who for ninety-three years, / Keeping the faith, believed you could get / Through the strait gate and the needle's eye if / You made up your mind straight and narrow" (FF, 249). Her physical disfigurement ("her wrenched back bent double, hunched over / The plank tied to the arms of her rocker / With a pillow on it to keep her head / Sideways up from her knees") suggests her disfigured soul. What Brunner calls "the blunt reality of actual family history, with its ancestors who could not be accommodated to Merwin's agenda for poetry,"[13] shows Merwin that he needs more distance before he can transform his family into myth. "The Drunk in the Furnace," the most powerful poem in the volume and his best single poem prior to *The Lice*, derives its powerful depiction of the milieu of Merwin's childhood from a character for whom there was no "real-life" model.

NOTES

9. Philip L. Gerber and Robert J. Gemmett, " 'Tireless Quest,' " 18.
10. Linda Trengen and Gary Storhoff, "Order and Energy in Merwin's *The Drunk in the Furnace*," 49.
11. Trengen and Storhoff, 49.

12. *Poetry as Labor and Privilege*, 78-81. Brunner says, "when Merwin, in England, questioned his ancestors, he had no idea what answers he would receive if they had been able to reply," but "soon after Merwin was back in America he set about finding information that would in fact produce nothing but answers," after which he is "encumbered with knowledge" (78).

13. *Poetry as Labor and Privilege*, 81.

—H.L. Hix, *Understanding W. S. Merwin* (Columbia: University of South Carolina Press, 1997): pp. 109–110.

CRITICAL ANALYSIS OF
"For the Anniversary
of My Death"

"For the Anniversary of My Death" is included in the 1967 collection, *The Lice*, a book which, with 1963's *The Moving Target*, is widely regarded as the major turning point in Merwin's stylistic approach to poetry. In both books, the poet uses virtually no punctuation of any sort, and his word choices are simpler, more fraught with abstraction as well as a sense of the universal. Still present in those collections is his fascination with death, ruination, the spiritual, and the natural, but it takes on a greater weight, ironically, as it is relieved of much of the formal girding of his earlier work.

"For the Anniversary of My Death" captures well all aspects of Merwin's style in the mid-1960s. The poem is presented in two irregular stanzas, but given the "hinge" between the first five-line stanza and the second, eight-line stanza, the poem suggests an inverted sonnet. The poem's only other holdover from more formal approaches is the persisting capitalization at the beginning of each line.

The poem starts out with the speaker telling the reader, "Every year without knowing it I have passed the day"—the longest single line/utterance in the poem. It sets out the situation. The line ends before he can specify which day it is, though the title tells us that it is the day which, in the future, will mark his death. He is aware that, for some, it will be an anniversary. For him, it is the day when "the last fires will wave to me/ And the silence will set out/ Tireless traveler/ Like the beam of a lightless star".

By making the last light a fire, the poet suggests something more timeless than a lamp or another more contemporary metaphor for life. The fire imagery is also primeval, and as such renders life more immediate and more mysterious at once, something more felt than understood. The same level of suggestion and abstraction operates in the other images as well. Death is a "silence," is "tireless" and thus inevitable, but something not easily explained. The "beam of a lightless star" is an abstraction, just as death is, just as is the notion that the speaker is living, again and again, the anniversary of something that has not yet happened, but is the only thing that surely *will* happen.

The speaker knows, however, that the abstractions and riddles of death will one day be known to him. "Then", he says, "I will no longer/ Find myself in life as in a strange garment". The line makes clear that, in addition to gaining clarity with death, the speaker currently does not understand life, or it does not fit him. Life, despite living it, is unfamiliar in a way. The speaker's view of death necessitates that it be a contrast to his current confusion. The phrases which follow indicate that his unfamiliarity is borne of surprise, "at the earth/ And the love of one woman/ And then shamelessness of men".

Critics have pointed out how Merwin's simple, emphatic, and consistent pairing of "the" with otherwise nonspecific nouns gives them a mythic specificity, enabling the reader's imagination to form the idea of whatever noun is presented. Thus, in addition to presenting "the last fires", "the silence", and "the earth", Merwin presents love as "the love of one woman" and the bird which follows, "the wren", such that they seem parts of a larger story, to merit such specific treatment. By assuming an awareness of just such a story, or the ability to imagine it, Merwin is able to have his poem resonate with a deeper level of story as implied by its language.

That sense of a missing influence powerfully informs the end of the poem. After the speaker relates that he will have clarity in death, he restates how confusing, how mysterious, is the life he currently lives.

He notes how he will, one day, not be "surprised", but by the point of the last three lines, he is offering a more-or-less concrete example of what engenders "surprise", with an example from the present moment. He is "writing after three days of rain/ Hearing the wren sing and the falling cease/ And bowing not knowing to what". Here, too, is the poet using "the" for effect. In particular, "the falling" is rendered specific as well as ambiguous. By writing it as *the* falling, Merwin limits the perception to less than it would be if he wrote simply "sing and falling cease", in which case one might have interpreted the phrase to mean any number of things falling, But, because of the presence of the article, the meaning can only be the aforementioned rain or an abstract falling, as what might be experienced in death. Because Merwin uses "the", the phrase operates almost as a pronoun, implying that he had referred to a specific kind of falling at another time.

It is a slightly different operation than that which works in the first stanza. In the first stanza, by referring to "the last fires" and "the silence" it works as though the speaker assumes we know that of which he speaks. That assumption implies a depth of story, or myth, under-girding the poem. It is that deep story which both surprises him and seems to promise him clarity, that uniting story of death.

The ambiguity of the rest of the poem, and its seeming dependence on some deeper but unstated story comes to its fullest power in the ultimate line of the poem. When the speaker is "bowing not knowing to what" he is responding to a presence in which he believes and in which he trusts, though, like the day which will be the anniversary, he cannot render tangible or specific. The quandary of the speaker is to be perpetually convinced of the presence of greater forces and to be perpetually ignorant of anything other than their existence. For Merwin, that paradox is a shaping force in much of his poetry, a body of work that insists on intimate and specific familiarity with the things of the world while admitting that what we *know* is much smaller than what we sense of understand as *being*.

CRITICAL VIEWS ON

"For the Anniversary
of My Death"

RICHARD HOWARD ON PROPHETIC VOICE

[In this second excerpt from his *Alone with America* essay, Richard Howard discusses the development of Merwin's prophetic voice.]

But even when Merwin speaks as a prophet out of his solitude into that opposing solitude which is Other People, as in "A Scale in May":

To succeed consider what is as though it were past
Deem yourself inevitable and take credit for it
If you find you no longer believe enlarge the temple

—even when he acknowledges Other Poets ("you who were haunted all your life by the best of you / hiding in your death"), there is a chill, almost a silence that lines his speech, and a difference about his notation of the world which I take as the final achievement of his vast mutations; it is the welcoming of his destitution among men in this book (as in the last it was the encompassing of his death in a private history) that sounds the special note of *The Lice*:

All morning with dry instruments
The field repeats the sound
Of rain
From memory ...
It is August
The flocks are beginning to form
I will take with me the emptiness of my hands
What you do not have you find everywhere

These lines are from a poem called "Provision," and if we recall that the word means, precisely, a looking ahead, a vision of the future, we can see that the poetry of this man has moved from preterition to presence to prophecy, and that it is, in its latest, mastered avatar, *provisional* in the proudest as well as the humblest sense, foreseeing and providing for its own metamorphosis; perhaps what I have called coolness and detachment is merely the effect of a poetry which has altogether committed itself to that encounter with identity we call, at our best, reality; for no poetry, where it is good, transcends anything or is about anything: it is itself, discovering its own purpose and naming its own meaning—its own provision, as Merwin provides it in "For the Anniversary of My Death":

> *Every year without knowing it I have passed the day*
> *When the last fires will wave to me*
> *And the silence will set out*
> *Tireless traveller*
> *Like the beam of a lightless star*
> *Then I will no longer*
> *Find myself in life as in a strange garment*
> *Surprised at the earth*
> *And the love of one woman*
> *And the shamelessness of men*
> *As today writing after three days of rain*
> *Hearing the wren sing and the falling cease*
> *And bowing not knowing to what*

> —Richard Howard, *Alone with America: Essays on the Art of Poetry in the United States since 1950* (New York: Atheneum, 1980): pp. 443–444.

CHERI DAVIS ON APOCALYPTIC DEJA-VU

[In this excerpt, Davis puts the poem in context with others from *The Lice*, to show Merwin's overall approach to discussing mortality.]

Any contemplation of the images of destruction and the depths of bitterness found in *The Lice* may lead an astute reader to conclude that Merwin is prophesying an apocalypse at hand. Jarold Ramsey addresses himself to this question: "In that primer of modern apocalyptics, *The Sense of an Ending*, Frank Kermode observes how the experience of *déjà vu* seems naturally to attend meditations on The End—an observation pertinent to Merwin's vision. The imagination baffled at its impulse to conceive images of a post-apocalyptic future becomes suffused with an uncanny sense that what is happening has all happened before."[24] It is this mentality that impels Merwin to write a poem "For the Anniversary of my Death" which opens "Every year without knowing it I have passed the day / When the last fires will wave to me / And the silence will set out / Tireless traveller / Like the beam of a lightless star" (L, 58). The "lightless star" is a constant image for any event whose significance he cannot fully fathom. Mystery and unfathomability also characterize the experience of *déjà vu*: one senses that something has occurred before but one cannot account for how, when, or why.

In fact, the mood, voice, and locus of *The Lice* are themselves *déjà vus*; all have appeared before in "Canso," published in 1954:

I will myself become
A Hades into which I can descend.

It will be a domain of déjà-vus,
The final most outlandish fastness of
Familiarity without memory,
Whose set dimensions, whose mode of privacy
And mode of pain I with my living breath
Shall enter, saying, "Like an Icarus
I have fallen into my shadow." There shall be seen
The death of the body walking in shapes of bodies
Departure's self hid in a guise of sojourn,
As it seems among the living. But on those hills
The shadows of sheep are folded, not the sheep
But on those lakes or the mirages of

Those lakes not birds are reflected, but the flight
Of birds across no sky. It is nevertheless
A place of recognition, though it be
Of recognition of nothing; a place of knowledge
Though it be knowledge of nothing; in this land
No landscape but a demeanor of distance
Where interchangeably the poles are death
And death, as in an opposition of mirrors
Where no beginning is, no end, I have lived
Not recognizing, for as long as knowledge. (F, 114–15)

These stanzas define the limits of the Hades of the self "into
which I can descend"—into which he *does* descend in *The Lice*.
There the polarity between death and death creates a static,
bodiless region where no substance, only shadow and mirage
exist: "Departure's self hid in the guise of sojourn." If the speaker
is Icarus, he represents fallen ambition. Death mirroring death in
timeless recognition provokes a "Familiarity without memory, /
Whose set dimensions, whose mode of privacy / And mode of
pain I ... Shall enter." The world of *The Lice* is a private and
painful hell: the cardinal experience is intimate "familiarity
without memory," an experience those in Dante's *Inferno* testify to
in their own "domain of déjà-vus." Although literally this is
Hades, it might just as well be an image of the end of time, the
apocalyptic diminishment T.S. Eliot records in *The Hollow Men*:
"This is the way the world ends / Not with a bang but a
whimper."

The lice or "bugs of regret" which live off the ghostly
presences inhabiting this world could be the prior life's
"unresolved alternatives, the frustrated purposes, the guilt,
missed chances, the unwritten poems of his discontinuous
lives."[25] To name an entity gives one ineluctable power over it,
yet none of these entities is precisely named or nameable by the
speaker. As demonstrated earlier regarding the poem "The
Animals," the first poem in *The Lice*, when "I with no voice" can
remember "names to invent for them," one may be won over and
return. Until the speaker can name it, its status will stay

unresolved and he will bring it along with him into the present and future. What one cannot name one cannot stand on equal footing with; it stays latent in the subconscious, it continues to bear witness to failure. Ghosts speak only when proffered the blood of remorse or grief:

New ghost is that what you are
Standing on the stairs of water

No longer surprised

Hope and grief are still our wings
Why we cannot fly

What failure still keeps you
Among us the unfinished

So opens the poem "Is That What You Are," the second poem in *The Lice*. Note that in the seventh line "we" are the "unfinished," not the ghost. And by implication, the "failure" mentioned in the line before is "ours" not his. Proof of this resides in the speaker's query and response: "Why are you there / I did not think I had anything else to give / The wheels say it after me." His weariness and sadness are apparent here. What we have missed resides with us in our houses and is all about us, riding on the very air we breathe. We look through it while "Standing on the stairs of water" or looking out the window each morning. Strange personages of whose existence we slowly become aware enter our rooms unsummoned: in an earlier poem "Witnesses" evening enters this way and "bats flower in the crevices / You and your brothers" (MT, 44). In "Evening" Merwin writes, "I look up but it is only / Evening again the old hat without a head / How long will it be till he speaks when he passes" (L, 51). They do not speak, and he cannot find the words to address them. Despair has moved in for good, and it clings, becoming a familiar inhabitant.

The dead do not question the futility of their lives, so why should the poet? In the outstanding poem "A Scale in May," he says:

Through the day the nameless stars keep passing the door
That have come all the way out of death
Without questions

The walls of light shudder and an owl wakes in the heart
I cannot call upon words
The sun goes away to set elsewhere

Before nightfall colorless petals blow under the door
And the shadows
Recall their ancestors in the house beyond death. (L, 50)

"I cannot call upon words" sums up the entire experience of *The Lice*. A penetrating wordless horror causes the light to shudder, "an owl wakes in the heart / ... The sun goes away to set elsewhere." And this "is the time when the beards of the dead get their growth." What recourse is there? A shocking knife image concludes "Is That What You Are," a symbol of deliverance and also danger: "And at the windows in the knives / You are watching." Knives are instruments of death as well as self-knowledge, probing insight as well as self-destruction. Seeing into the mirror they provide, seeing through their "watching" eyes may enable the speaker to penetrate the obscurity of the self and find then the words "to invent for them." He may seize the opportunity to communicate with these ghosts and dispel them by eliminating their reason for existence. "Hope and grief are still our wings," but "why we cannot fly" he does not know. Though "I did not think I had anything else to give," to find what he has to give would be to solve the riddle of the lice, and thus to achieve self-transcendence. As one of the sayings of Antonio Porchia that Merwin was translating around this time goes: "No one understands that you have given everything. You must give more."[26] Without the cleaving potential of the knife his frozen consciousness can only "remember that I am falling / That I am the reason / And that my words are the garment of what I shall never be / Like the tucked sleeve of a one-armed boy."

A final experience of *déjà vu* in the last lines of the book confirms the saving potential of recognition, remembrance, and waking to the call of the present:

> In the dark while the rain fell
> The gold chanterelles pushed through a sleep that was not mine
>
> Waking me
> So that I came up the mountain to find them
> Where they appear it seems I have been before
> I recognize their haunts as though remembering
> Another life
>
> Where else am I walking even now
> Looking for me

If lives are exchangeable, so are griefs. If "I" can be walking experiencing "their haunts as though remembering / Another life," another "I" could be walking "Looking for me." This poignant process wakes the seeker of "gold chanterelles" up from his bed of ash. He rises and walks and is healed.

In a critical discussion of the future of poetry, published in *The Distinctive Voice* (1966), Merwin asserts that poetry is now facing extinction just as certainly as the pupfish or any of the vanishing species: "But then, among my peculiar failings is an inability to believe that the experience of being human, that gave rise to the arts in the first place, can continue to be nourished in a world contrived and populated by nothing but humans."[27] He fears that poetry itself may be merely vestigial or atavistic in an age when our lives are lived wholly apart from animals and our kinship with other forms of life is attenuated or nonexistent; thus it is fitting, that in "Looking for Mushrooms at Sunrise," the non-human world ventures into his consciousness, warns him, rouses him:

When it is not yet day
I am walking on centuries of dead chestnut leaves
In a place without grief
Though the oriole
Out of another life warns me That I am awake (L, 80)

He perceives a voice "Out of another life" while "walking on centuries of dead chestnut leaves." The leaves, symbols of the eternal recycling and recurrence of lives, participate in communication with him like the oriole who warns him out of another life "That I am awake." The leaves dispel grief, pointing as they do to the potential of other existences for the poet. Heightened awareness of other dimensions in our own lives and consciousnesses derives from close attention to nature. Lives as simple as those of the "gold chanterelles" can push through one's sleep and impel one to "recognize their haunts as though remembering / Another life." To remain open to such experience, Merwin implies, is to draw on the resources and strengths of former—and even future—lives; this seems all the more necessary in a fallen, disrupted time.

The poem ends in acute awareness that another higher self is "walking even now / Looking for me." Does despair prompt him to rationalize the existence of another "I" who searches for him? Or is the ending merely an exquisite aesthetic flourish, a gesture to make the poem "work"? A quantity of evidence drawn from his next three books of poetry, *The Carrier of Ladders*, *Writings to an Unfinished Accompaniment*, and *The Compass Flower*, substantiates the fact that in the 1970s Merwin was newly receptive to other dimensions of consciousness, other non-human voices in nature, and other ways of perceiving the life cycle. In "Words from a Totem Animal" in *The Carrier of Ladders*, he writes, "Send me out into another life / lord because this one is growing faint / I do not think it goes all the way" (19).

Merwin mourns the fact that today poetry and the animals are being relegated to an inferior position. For him they embody a dimension of spiritual life that is being lost: both are like "that Biblical waif ... the spirit. No one has any claims on it, no one deserves it, no one knows where it goes. It is not pain, and it is not the subconscious, though it can hail from either as though it were at home there." In order to keep the spirit alive, despite difficult, even desperate times, he will continue to write, for "absolute despair has no art, and I imagine the writing of a poem, in whatever mode, still betrays the existence of hope, which is why poetry is more and more chary of the conscious mind, in our age." The reflection of conscious mind can only lead him to despair: rational, logical examination of history militates against his feeling any hope for the future. Still, he asserts, "what the poem manages to find hope for may be part of what it keeps trying to say."[28] What Merwin said of the small bird in "The Room" might be said of the spirit and voice of *The Lice*: "You would say it was dying it is immortal."

Notes

24. *Massachusetts Review*, 14: 572.
25. Ibid., p. 585.
26. *Voices*, p. 31.
27. "Notes for a Preface," *The Distinctive Voice*, ed. William J. Martz (Glenview, Ill., 1966), p. 269.
28. Ibid., all quotations in this passage are from p. 272.

—Cheri Davis, *W.S. Merwin* (Boston: Twayne Publishers, 1981): pp. 98–103.

MARK CHRISTHILF ON MERWIN'S IDEA OF LIFE AS TEMPORARY CONDITION

[Mark Christhilf is Professor of English at Eastern Illinois University. He is the author of *W.S. Merwin the Mythmaker*. In the excerpt, from the chapter, "A Mythic Image of Humankind," Christhilf contends that mortal existence, for Merwin, is an anomalous period of time spent away from a being's "original condition."]

Mortal existence in Merwin's tale is objectification—a fall from the original condition of freedom and spirit. At birth each person takes on a body, becoming subject to the limitations and necessities of objective being in time. Yet each remembers the original freedom by virtue of imagination, which for Merwin is the spiritual part of the human being. As though it were a piece of the original freedom, imagination continues to touch the source of existence, to conceive the possibility of immortal being. For this reason each person lives a divided life, having both mortal identity and immortal being. On several occasions in his career Merwin characterizes mankind's divided nature, reformulating the traditional human duality of body and spirit. Stressing mortal identity as contingency in nature and immortal being as creative imagination, Merwin claims in his essay on Dylan Thomas that the human being is "man the creature-creator" ("The Religious Poet," 63); later, in "Notes for a Preface," he refers to "man, the animal and the artist" (272). Like Wallace Stevens, Merwin regards imagination as the supreme faculty—the divinity in each human being.

In Merwin's story mortal existence is a span of time after which one returns to the original condition. At the end of life one encounters death not as a total annihilation of identity but rather as a return to life at the level of immortal being. Merwin imagines his own death in these terms in his well-known poem in *The Lice*, "For the Anniversary of My Death." On the day of death, he claims, his life will be extinguished as if it were one flame in a universe of fire; but part of him will continue, setting out like a "Tireless traveller / Like the beam from a lightless star." Merwin also imagines death as reunification: in death one rejoins the community of spirit composed of ancestors who preceded one on the earth. In "Wharf," in *Writings to an Unfinished Accompaniment*, he describes the experience of death as both an end and a beginning in which one recovers an original unity:

... our gravestones are blowing
like clouds backward
through time to find us
they sail over us through us

back to lives that waited
for us
and we never knew. (38)

For Merwin the dead play an important role in the individual's mortal existence. Even in this life communication with them is both necessary and possible. This motif brings to light the traditional emphases in his story, and in fact he is repeatedly inspired by premodern conceptions of death and afterlife. Death, for tribal peoples, is not an event in which the spirit goes far away to another land or heaven. Rather, the spirit remains near the community of the living either waiting to reenter a body being born or lurking in trees or clouds, where it serves as an intercessor for its mortal relatives. Just on the other side of the appearances of things, the dead ask for favors (such as rain) from the great, untreated god who remains a mystery.[1] In Merwin's story the dead exist within and behind things—in the creative dimension of depth—and he uses the motif of walls or doors to indicate their separation from their mortal brethren..

NOTE

1. See Hartley Burr Alexander, *The Mythology of All Races: North American* (New York: Cooper Square, 1964), 190.

—Mark Christhilf, *W.S. Merwin the Mythmaker* (Columbia: University of Missouri Press, 1986): pp. 62–63.

MARJORIE PERLOFF ON ORDER IN THE POEM

[Marjorie Perloff is one of the leading critics of our time. She is the author of many books, including *Rhyme and Meaning in the Poetry of Yeats*, *The Poetic Art of Robert Lowell*, *Frank O'Hara: Poet Among Painters*, *The Futurist Moment: Avant-Garde, Avant-Guerre, and the Language of Rupture*, *Poetic License: Studies in Modernist and Postmodernist Lyric*, *Radical Artifice: Writing Poetry in the Age of Media*, and *Wittgenstein's Ladder: Poetic Language and the Strangeness of the Ordinary*. She is Sadie Dernham Patek Professor of Humanities at Stanford University. In this section from her essay "Merwin and the Sorrows of Literary History," Perloff explains the difference in technique of this poem from Merwin's earlier, more typically Modernist work.]

Unlike Beckett, to whom he has frequently been compared,[17] Merwin rarely invents a fictional situation in which emptiness, darkness, the failure of the language to mirror "reality" are actually *experienced* by someone. It is time to look at a concrete example.

FOR THE ANNIVERSARY OF MY DEATH

Every year without knowing it I have passed the day
When the last fires will wave to me
And the silence will set out
Tireless traveller
Like the beam of a lightless star

Then I will no longer
Find myself in life as in a strange garment
Surprised at the earth
And the love of one woman
And the shamelessness of men
As today writing after three days of rain
Hearing the wren sing and the falling cease
And bowing not knowing to what

(L, 58)

Karl Malkoff, who calls this "one of the most striking poems in the collection [*The Lice*]," provides an analysis which is worth pondering:

The central idea of the poem is simple: each year contains the date on which the poet will finally die, each year he unknowingly passes the anniversary of his death. But the implications of this premise are complex. They involve nothing less than the total breakdown of conventional modes of apprehending time. Viewing time *sub specie aeternitatis* ... Merwin labels the linear sense of time—that is, time as inexorable, unfolding, continual movement—as illusory. The "beam of a lightless star" is in one sense a metaphor of Merwin's own language of silence, the silence of death, the silence of meaninglessness. A beam emanating from a lightless star also suggests that from a sufficiently detached perspective, a dead star can appear still alive.... This is a fine symbol of the poet's eternal longings. And it is a fine symbol of time as relative in a world of absolute being.

Merwin perceives that his death has already taken place in precisely the sense that the present exists eternally. The temporal distinction is false. In the second stanza, however, he sets up new distinctions to replace the old. He will no longer "Find myself in life as in a strange garment." He will lose his divisive perceptions that isolate him from the rest of being. Merwin's response is characteristically ambivalent. He will no longer be "surprised at the earth / And the love of one woman." The uncomfortable world of time and change is also the realm of specifically human satisfactions. It is finally to this human universe that Merwin must return. (pp. 214–15)

I have cited this reading at such length because it strikes me as wholly typical of what we might call a sixties reading of sixties poetry. What Malkoff goes on to call "the hallmark of Merwin's 'new style'" is that his images consist "not of detailed description, but rather of actions and essential types." Indeed, the types become "almost allegorical.... But like all modern allegory, it is not supported by an ordered universe; it is grounded in nothingness" (p. 215). Here Malkoff unwittingly contradicts his own reading of the text, for what he has just shown, painstakingly and convincingly, is that Merwin's allegory, far from being "grounded in nothingness," is grounded in the familiar paradox that time is at once linear and eternal. "Viewing time *sub specie aeternitatis*," the linear view is illusory, as the symbolic "beam" of the lightless star, shining millions of miles from its dead source, suggests. On the other hand, to lose one's linear sense of time is, as the poet says in the second stanza, to lose one's humanity, one's ability to be "surprised at the earth / And the love of one woman." A paradox as neat as any Cleanth Brooks discovered in Wordsworth's "It Is a Beauteous Evening" or Yeats's "Among School Children." Yeats, for that matter, had pondered a similar time/eternity paradox as early as "The Stolen Child."

How, then, is the poem different from the late modernist lyric of the fifties, including Merwin's own early work? For one thing, the "I" is not a persona but quite simply the poet himself—here is a point of departure that seemed much more striking to readers of the sixties than it does to us today. For another, the imagery does not have the texture of W.K. Wimsatt's "concrete universal," of the metaphysical conceit dear to the New Critics. Merwin's language is "simple," if by simple we mean familiar: everyone knows what "day" means, or "fire" or "silence" or "traveller" or "three days of rain." It is also curiously abstract: most of the generic nouns are preceded by an article but not by an adjectival modifier: "the day," "the silence," "the earth," "the beam," "the love," "the shamelessness." In the rare cases when the noun does have a modifier, the adjective works to increase the sense of abstraction—"the tireless traveller," "strange garment," "last fires," "lightless star." Accordingly, the landscape of the poem seems to be mysterious; it has repeatedly been called "dreamlike" or "surreal," even though both these terms are probably misnomers: in a dream, one doesn't think in terms of "Every year" or "Then I will no longer / Find myself" or "today writing after three days of rain"; and "surreal" refers, not to something vaguely mysterious and blurred, but to a landscape, whether in the verbal or the visual arts, in which objects, people, actions, or situations that cannot conceivably coexist in the "real world" are brought together, as in Magritte's painting *Collective Invention* (in which a fish with the lower torso and legs of a woman—a sort of reverse mermaid—is seen lying on a naturalistically painted beach beside the ocean).

But whatever term we use to describe Merwin's images, it is true that they are unlike, say, John Crowe Ransom's metaphors in "The Equilibrists." If "Lemuel's Blessing" is, as Paul Carroll argues, again a poem built around a single paradox ("one who is an archetype of civilized tribal values petitions in a traditionally communal form of prayer that he be allowed to exist outside of civilized communal values ... and come to share as deeply as possible the nature and characteristics of the wolf" pp. 146–47), that paradox is nevertheless framed differently from Ransom's, an allegorical mode having replaced the symbolist mode of the moderns. This difference aside, Merwin's poetry carried on the tradition of the well-made poem of the fifties. For what distinguishes a poem like "For the Anniversary of My Death" from the "undecidable" texts of a Beckett on the one hand, as from its modernist predecessors on the other, is the marked authorial control that runs counter to the lipservice paid to "bowing not knowing to what." Far from being a poem of *discovery*, a text whose "echo repeats no sound," "For the Anniversary of My Death" is characterized by a strong sense of closure.

Consider, for example, the stanzaic division. The first stanza (five lines) describes what happens "Every year"; the second (eight lines) refers to "Then" (when I will be dead). The first concentrates on the silence of eternity, beyond "the last fires," the eternity symbolized by the beam of the lightless star. The second recalls, even as does the final stanza of Yeats's "The Stolen Child," what will be lost when death ends the inexorable forward movement of time, when the "strange garment" of life is shed: namely, the love of one woman, the shamelessness of men, the singing of the wren, the falling of rain, and, yes, the "bowing not knowing to what," which is to say, "bowing" to the premonition of death one has in moments of transition, as when a three-day rain comes to an end.

Does the language. "mock the poet with its absences"? Not really, or at least its mockery seems to take place only on the surface. The first line quickly gives the game away: since there is obviously no way to know on what day of the year one will die, the phrase "without knowing it" strikes a rather self-important note. This is the language, not of dream or of mysterious Otherness, but of calculation: the setting up of a hypothetical situation that brings the time/eternity paradox into sharp relief. Again, the reference to "death" as the moment when "the last fires will wave to me" seems to me the very opposite of "spare" (a word regularly applied to Merwin's poetry by his admirers); it is a gestural, a decorative metaphor reminiscent of Dylan Thomas rather than René Char.[18] Indeed, lines 2–5, with their heavy alliteration and assonance, their repetition and slow, stately movement, have the authentic Thomas ring:

When the last fires will wave to me
And the silence will set out Tireless traveller
Like the beam of a lightless star

The language of the second stanza is increasingly abstract, conceptual, formulaic, recalling, as Bloom points out, the conservative rhetoric of poets like Longfellow or MacLeish. To call life "a strange garment," to define one's humanity in terms of "the love of one woman" and the need to wrestle with "the shamelessness of men"—such locutions have the accent of the Sunday sermon rather than the surrealist lyric. Given this context, the "bowing not knowing to what" in the unpunctuated last line is a predictable closural device: it points us back to the title with its recognition that one of the days now lived through will, one year, be the day of the poet's death.

NOTES

17. See Nelson, "Resources of Failure," p. 90; Robert Peters, *The Great American Poetry Bake-Off* (Metuchen, N.J.: Scarecrow Press, 1979), pp. 259, 267.

18. For the Char connection, see Howard, *Alone with America*, p. 435, and cf. Altieri, *Enlarging the Temple*, p. 196: "Merwin is so disturbing in large measure because his roots are European—in poets like Rilke and Follain who have developed numerous variations on the *via negativa* as the way of enduring presence." It should be noted that Altieri's discussion of Merwin, although not published before *Enlarging the Temple* (1979), was framed, as are the other chapters in the book, prior to 1970.

—Marjorie Perloff, "Merwin and the Sorrows of Literary History." *W.S. Merwin: Essays on the Poetry*, Cary Nelson and Ed Folsom, eds. (Urbana: University of Illinois Press, 1987): pp. 132–135.

Edward J. Brunner on the Poem's Merger of Future and Past

[Brunner describes in this excerpt how the poem maintains separate times and tenses in the consciousness of the poem.]

It is significant that this first person is a mourner who has no one for whom to mourn, because Merwin's return to a community will hinge upon his understanding that if one can learn to mourn oneself, one can begin to mourn for others.

Merwin's own act of mourning himself occurs in "For the Anniversary of My Death," a work that opens in the realm of immense abstractions, with Merwin positing that "every year without knowing it I have passed the day / When the last fires will wave to me." Like the enormity of the sun, this cosmic view is appalling in its undeniability and in its emptiness, but here it gives rise to its opposite, an urgent wish to embrace the earth, a longing to honor even the smallest of moments as though they were utterly significant: "As today writing after three days of rain / Hearing the wren sing and the falling cease / And bowing not knowing to what." The renewal as rainfall ends is magnified, transforming the wren's song into a celebration both modest and all-embracing. The rest of *The Lice* flowers out of this grief-stricken understanding that no reference to death can be allowed that does not in some way include one's own loss of all that is beloved. Moreover, what is truly beloved is yet to be discovered: what one honors, at this moment, is unknown—one bows "not knowing to what."

"For the Anniversary of My Death" is one of a number of poems that hold out an opportunity to reverse the course of events. Sometimes that opportunity is dismissed as unlikely: in "When the War is Over" Merwin insists that "we will all enlist again," having learned nothing at all. In "The Finding of Reasons" and "For a Coming Extinction" he writes with certainty of a future that holds out no promise at all. But in "Come Back" he imagines a reunion-only he confesses that he had held back, as one paralyzed, "until you were gone." The gift of renewal is sought out now that it may be too late. Merwin cannot shake off this constant awareness that it may be too late, even as this future that is "dead / And our own" is offered so it may not come about.

The Lice is finally so impressive not because of Merwin's righteous anger at the imperfections of the human world but because of his tenderness toward those imperfections. Writing fiercely of alienation and despair in the opening pages of the book, then writing delicately of the natural world and its purity in the central pages, Merwin combines all he has learned in "Avoiding News by the River." Before the sky "fills with blood," before humans awake, the world exists in intricate concord. Stars hide while warblers hunt and trout rise as light flows—events not directly related to one another even as they effortlessly harmonize. When humans awake, all turns problematic:

In an hour it will be summer
I dreamed that the heavens were eating the earth
Waking it is not so
Not the heavens (L, 68)

The future tense appears in this stanza, distinguishing us, who mark off time in segments and give names to seasons and conceive a direction for the future, from the creatures. Our intelligence sets us apart from other species, but our responsibilities increase proportionately. We should expect to know what we are doing.

That demand complicates the second stanza, dissolving the harmonies present before dawn. Our intelligence should lead us to recognize that it is not the heavens eating the earth, not some natural catastrophe over which there can be no control: that is only a dream from which we must awaken. And awakened, we stand further distinguished from creatures essentially innocent: the murders of the wren and the dinners of the badger are no cause for shame, for creatures act as they must, without awareness beyond the moment. Our problem is that we do not distinguish ourselves enough, as the phrase "worldly good" suggests. For the wren and badger, their motive is survival. For us, gifted with intelligence, living should be more than survival—it should be burdened with responsibility, with care for others, which is why we are given to feel a shame absent from the natural world turning in its self-sufficient unity. Yet the thrust of the poem, with the convoluted syntax of the last line—two negatives from which we must deduce a positive—points to how heavy a burden that intelligence can be. The burden of intelligence is anguish, a division from the wholeness of nature—as the logic of the "if–then" of the final line weighs ponderously on the entire work, grinding it to a dead stop.

Intelligence, as Merwin conceives it, must not become power because its strength is too enormous; our distance from other creatures is simply too great. The check on that power is nothing less than our shame, which is the state into which we fall when our awareness singles us out as the interloper with enormous powers. To endure that sudden arrest of our inherent authority is the problem Merwin comes to appreciate in the course of *The Lice*. On the one hand, it is natural for us to overstep our bounds, to press beyond our limits. That is the elemental use of the intelligence, especially when placed in the service of technical feats. On the other hand, what is harder to realize, because it contravenes our techniques for managing matters, is that the intelligence can also measure its limits—that the ability to imagine the future is given to prevent us from yielding thoughtlessly to our power. To conceive of an apocalyptic future can become a self-negating prophecy; the conception affirms the mind as it serves in its own preservation, using its strength to know when to limit its power.

—Edward J. Brunner, *Poetry as Labor and Privilege: The Writings of W.S. Merwin* (Urbana: University of Illinois Press, 1991): pp. 149–151.

[Michael W. Thomas, at the time the article was written, was on faculty at Malvern Girls' College, Worcestershire, England. Thomas' explication argues that the poem has a rational character to its thought.]

The speaker of Merwin's two-stanza poem "For the Anniversary of My Death"[1] ponders from an uncommon angle the notion that death exists in life's midst: "Every year without knowing it," he begins, "I have passed the day / When the last fires will wave to me" (lines 1–2). There is a paradox in these lines. Living his way through the calendar, the speaker professes ignorance about the date of his death. Admittedly, he cannot pinpoint this—nor can anyone, without benefit of psychic help. But his declaration suggests that he approaches each and every day with the knowledge that, in some future year, it could mark his departure from life. Thus, though certainty eludes him, he knows full well that he has passed that fateful day. Consequently his tone conveys his respect for all his days and indeed for time itself, the mortal experience of which is necessarily defined by the timelessness of death.

The remainder of the poem elaborates the observation in the opening lines. The speaker views departure from life as a verity which is best confronted through elemental imagery. Hence, "the last fires," with their waving motion, become for him symbols of mankind's final contact with that vibrancy separating the quick from the dead. The waving of the fires, however, introduces another paradox. Initial readings of the poem might suggest that the fires are offering the dying mortal (the speaker's future self) a valediction. However, they could also be taunting him: their haphazard waving demonstrates, even flaunts, that energy which, in due course, the speaker will no longer command.

The speaker then offers another image of his grim anniversary. On that day, he says,

the silence will set out
Tireless traveler
Like the beam of a lightless star (3–5)

Here, the element obliquely referred to is air: through it—or more generally, through the open firmament—the "beam" of death will travel in chilling silence. "[A] lightless star" is another paradox, implying that the speaker's mortal energy, previously figured in the waving fires, will only survive as a concept defined by its antithesis, extinction. Yet another phrase in the above lines suggests the speaker's attempt, desperate though it may seem, to infuse the notion of approaching death with his present vitality: the silence of his death will be a "Tireless traveler." The adjective "tireless" is most commonly used to describe human endeavor, to distinguish those who possess drive and vision from those who do not. Admittedly, "tireless" is equally applicable to death's unique energy, its cold persistence through the ages. But it is strongly arguable that, discomfited by the mockery of the waving fires in line two, the speaker seeks to present death's unending journey as an extension of human power, specifically his own.

The first stanza ends at this point, and it seems that the pause between stanzas one and two signifies the speaker's searching reflection on his previous thoughts. When next he speaks, his attitude toward death appears to have changed. He no longer responds to it with a mixture of unease and awe. Indeed his words now suggest an absorption in the notion of death that draws him toward that state, away from life's vitality: "Then I will no longer / Find myself in life as in a strange garment" (6–7). Equating life with strangeness, the speaker challenges the usual idea that quotidian life is dependable and (a much abused word) "real," while death and what it portends are enigmatic and thus frightening. He extends this equation in line eight. Once dead, he says, he will no longer be "Surprised at the earth." This elemental reference communicates three levels of meaning. First, it suggests the speaker's astonishment at, and fascination with, the very fact of that element's existence; and the earth as element, solid and unyielding, does indeed seem at odds with the concept of the earth as celestial body, spinning unsupported in a seeming void. Second, assuming a broader definition of "earth," line eight implies the speaker's surprise at the diversity of stimuli, both human and nonhuman, on earth. Third, extending the second level of meaning, the reference to the earth suggests that the speaker is so astonished at the variety of life that, observing it, he finds it alien to his own experience.

This reaction typifies the emotional state of those on the verge of death: an imminent parting from life can, by all accounts, make the familiar seem strange. This level of meaning emphasizes the frame of mind in which, after the pause between stanzas, the speaker resumes his meditations. He is close to death insofar as he explores the changes wrought upon his sense of life by the close consideration of dying. His frame of mind here recalls Nick Carraway's assessment of Jay Gatsby's mood, shortly before the latter's death:

> He must have looked up at an unfamiliar sky through frightening leaves and shivered as he found what a grotesque thing a rose is and how raw the sunlight was upon the scarcely created grass. A new world, material without being real....[2]

Gatsby is still very much alive; but he is also enduring the death of his hopes regarding Daisy Buchanan, an experience that for him is not far removed from death itself. Moments later, George Wilson's gun changes that intimation of death into a reality.

In lines nine and ten, Merwin's speaker elaborates his thoughts on the earth, particularizing aspects that surprise him: "... the love of one woman / And the shamelessness of men." For him, these eternal human characteristics are now strands in the "strange garment" of life (7). A mind uninfluenced by death would not respond thus to them.

By the end of stanza two, the speaker has clearly accepted his approaching death. The poem's final three lines are as follows:

As today writing after three days of rain
Hearing the wren sing and the falling cease
And bowing not knowing to what (11–13)

"As today" yields two meanings when read in the context of
the whole stanza, particularly "Then I will no longer / Find
myself in life as in a strange garment" (6–7). It could simply be
taken to emphasize the speaker's sense of alienation from
quotidian life, his surprise "at the earth" (8), at the power of
monogamous love, and (in contrast) at the suspect morality of
mankind. Though he has pondered these things often, the phrase
implies, they have never engaged his mind more strongly than
"today."

"As today" also contains a more forceful meaning, one that
challenges the first. As it is also demonstrably on his mind, the
concept of death may suddenly have superseded his feelings
about the earth. "[T]oday"—or at that precise moment—he may
no longer find himself "in life as in a strange garment," because
all thoughts on that subject, of whatever nature, have vanished. If
this latter meaning is accepted, it follows that he has embraced
the fact of death, allowing it to carry him far beyond mortal
concerns.

The rest further emphasizes the idea that though still a
sentient being, the speaker is swathed, as it were, in death. He is
"writing after three days of rain" (11). This phrase suggests that
the rain (which, though symbolizing earthly life, can also oppress
and disturb) has hitherto prevented him from exploring and
absorbing the fact of death. Now, however, its cessation leaves
him free to do so. He hears "the wren sing and the falling cease"
(12). Frequently associated with winter, death's season, the wren
appropriately takes the place of the rain.[3] Whereas "the falling"
represents nourishment and renewal, the wren's song hymns
death's inevitability, underscoring the speaker's acceptance of it.
He thus finds himself involuntarily "bowing not knowing to
what" (13).

A final paradox occurs here, recalling the opening of stanza
one. As discussed above, the speaker commences by saying he

does not know which day will mark the anniversary of his death. Nonetheless, he is intensely aware that each day of the year is that anniversary *in potentia*; as the tone of his words suggests— and as the whole poem makes clear—he treats each day as such. Now, at the end of the poem, he declares ignorance about the reason for his bow. However, given his increasing engagement with the fact of death, together with the setting of wren-song and the silence after rain, it is strongly arguable that "today" is the anniversary on which he has pondered for so long. Intuition, rather than conscious knowledge, has lodged that truth in his mind, and his bow acknowledges that fact. Moreover, no punctuation closes the stanza. Though punctuation is absent from the whole poem, its absence is especially important here. It suggests an abrupt end to the speaker's train of thought. In consequence, what could be called the silence on the page, after his final word, stresses appropriately his submission to the notion of death.

Thus, "For the Anniversary of My Death" charts one mind's progress from anxiety to acquiescence in the face of death. Disturbed by the waving fires, symbols of the vitality he must relinquish, the speaker initially sees the silent journey of his death as the act of a "Tireless traveler" (4), continuing and thus affirming his present humanity. But in stanza two, his attitude changes markedly. At first, mentally approaching the verge of death, he finds that the quotidian round becomes, for him, an alien concept. However, given the second, more forceful connotation of "As today" (11), it seems that death subsequently cancels his sense of life's strangeness. As a result, at the end of the poem, he is far removed from any view of—or concern for—what surrounds him. From this novel standpoint, he unwittingly honors his somber anniversary.

As can also be seen, the direction taken by the speaker's thoughts is marked, at several crucial points, by images that draw upon the elements. In stanza one, the references to fire and air underscore the speaker's reluctance to surrender his mortal strengths. In stanza two, however, the images of earth and rain enforce his new perception of death as an acceptable, even comforting certainty. And it is to Merwin's credit that such a change of mind appears rational instead of fatalistic, dignified instead of cheaply sinister.

NOTES

1. W.S. Merwin, "For the Anniversary of My Death," *The Norton Anthology of Poetry*, ed. Alexander W. Allison et al., rev. shorter ed. (New York: Norton, 1975) 604. All references to the poem are from this edition.

2. F. Scott Fitzgerald, *The Great Gatsby* (New York, 1925; rpt. Middlesex: Penguin, 1986) 153–54.

3. I find particular support in British folklore for the connection between winter and the wren. On December 26, there used to occur "the hunting of the wren." The bird was caught and killed, and its hunters would then place it in a decorated casket and carry it from house to house, offering its feathers as good luck charms in exchange for money or food. I am indebted to Mr. Eric Payne, Worcestershire folklorist, for this information.

—Michael W. Thomas, "Merwin's 'For the Anniversary of My Death.'" *The Explicator* 49:2 (1991): pp. 126–129.

"The River of Bees"

"The River of Bees" is one of a number of elegiac poems in *The Lice*, and one which resonates with the epigraph from Herclitus with which Merwin begins the book:

> All men are deceived by the appearance of things, even Homer himself, who was the wisest man in Greece; for he was deceived by boys catching lice: they said to him, "What we have caught and what we have killed we have left behind, but what has escaped us we bring with us."

In the epigraph, the boys return bearing only what they cannot find. Many of the speakers in Merwin's poems bear the same things, as does the speaker of "For the Anniversary of My Death." That the lice are pathogenic and parasitic feeds the despairing tone Merwin develops in the collection; even the harmful things we conquer leave behind many more and worse. In many ways, "The River of Bees" concerns itself with what cannot be found but which lives with us and within us, the future, and ways of living.

The poem opens "In a dream," signaling that the reader might expect something of an order apart from reality. While Merwin plays much with the possibilities afforded by subjective reality, this poem's dream is of a recollected reality, thereby mixing dream and reality. Marjorie Perloff has stated explicitly that, by the time of *The Moving Target* and *The Lice* the "I" in Merwin's work was no longer a persona, but had become the poet himself, struggling with despair, reality, and a persistent apocalyptic vision. The critics included with this analysis implicitly concur. As a result, "The River of Bees" can be read as one of the most personal poems of a very personal collection.

In his dream, Merwin "returned to the river of bees," an image at once surreal and sonorous, carrying with it the likely drone of thousands. In the next line, we learn of "Five orange trees by the bridge," suggesting the possibility that bees hovered about the blossoms and the sticky fruit in late summer, by the water below, making thus a river of bees, and the description is a bit of imaginative lyricism. However, due to Merwin's now trademark absence of punctuation, it could just as well be an image to be taken at face value, as part of a dream. His "house" is "Beside two mills," and into the "courtyard a blind man followed/ The goats and stood singing/ Of what was older".

The blind man is, to most critics, Homeric. As he is singing, a form of versifying, and is singing of the past, he cannot be Tyresius. "The goats" carry with them associations with satyrs and agrarianism, and their presence with the man suggests a possible playfulness in him. But as the poem moves into another stanza, and the speaker says, "Soon it will be fifteen years" the line could be read as meaning that the incident occurred fifteen years ago, or that the dream occurred fifteen years ago. The following line suggests the former: "He was old he will have fallen into his eyes".

However, the line does more than locate the incident. The line dismisses the incident as one of little consequence, especially now. The man was old, Merwin tells himself, and has likely caved in on his uselessness, his sightless eyes. The line signals the beginning of a sort of argument the poet has with either a more cynical version of himself, or the voice of another being altogether, a prophet, as is suggested by Brunner's reading. Whichever it is, the new voice discounts the man and the arrogance of seeking meaning or elevation in life's fruitless enterprise.

The first voice returns in the next stanza: "I took my eyes/ A long way to the calendars/ Room after room asking how shall I live". It is the first inanimate, manmade thing to which the speaker looks for some sense of how to live. The voice, inspired by the blind man, seeks guidance, however, not from the man who sings of time gone by. He looks with his eyes, eyes which, unlike the blind man's, see. And he looks ahead, at calendars, at the yet to come, the weeks and months stretching into the future. He has calendars in every room, and he asks them how he shall live, as if in the time to come and the appointments and the blank and similar order of all that lies ahead, there will be an answer.

The next stanza begins, "One of the ends is made of streets". But, it is unclear to what the end finishes. Is the end of a way to live, as the line before intimates? Is it an end to the dream, to the song? The possibility for multiple meanings draws ambiguity into the poem, ambiguity that is both a hallmark of Merwin and a complicating part of the poem. The end, whether to a song, to the answer of a life philosophy, or to the dream, addresses the central concern of the poem. However, because it could end a song or a dream, it allows Merwin to dismiss it, whereas if it is the ultimate answer to a life philosophy, it would be harder for him to maintain the dual conversation of the poem.

As for the image itself, the streets have on them "One man processions" which "carry through it" (the end) "Empty bottles their/ Image of hope/ It was offered to me by name". The contrast between "one man" and "procession" gives a false gravity, consistent with the sneering voice of the prophet, to a man merely walking. As processions usually accompany wakes, funerals, weddings, and other life transitions, the visual of them with their "Image of hope" conveys upon it the feel of transition, as if realizing that the "empty bottle" meant that hope was nothing, non-existent, with a frame around it that, perhaps, is transparent. Merwin notes that the particular image of hope was offered to him, by its name, a name he does not include. Readers can infer that he does not remember it, or that it does not matter. But by implying that it had a name, he implies its age, its mythic existence in another time, another place, and that it has lost the relevance that would have made him remember its name.

In the next stanza, he stresses how "Once once and once/ In the same city I was born/ Asking what shall I say". Either he is emphatic about his single birth, or his birth was a trinity of sorts. Given Merwin's drift away from religion, the trinity is unlikely, but present, noteworthy because the other prominent numbers are multiples of five. The effect of the line, however, is the emphasis of once, but, because the next line stresses "In the same city," it is possible he means that he was born thrice, in three different times, in the same place, and so is irrevocably sentenced to live the same way, the same life, searching for the way to do it, and still ending up the same way. The sense of futility is powerful, and building, by this point of the meditation.

He reminds himself again, in the next stanza, that the old man "will have fallen into his mouth," this time having the singer's death center on the source of the song, the source of the doubt which first plagued the poet, wondering how to go forward and live a life worthy of remembered glories in the past. The man's memories "of what was older" have died with him, as have old ways. The cynical voice carps, "Men think they are better than grass," implying that the arrogance which seeks a "way" forgets that the lives of things are not intentional; they just are. The implication is that men are simply creations, biological entities that are just as likely as grass to exist at a certain time in a certain place. The statement denies most religious sense of natural "order" or hierarchy, and borders on atheistic, at least insomuch as it denies a willful deity with a "plan" for his creations.

Yet, Merwin's soul cannot let it rest at that dismissal: "I return to his voice rising like a forkful of hay" and hay, of course, is dead, cut grass. Hay is rendered by the work of men, and is pitched with the tools they make, for purposes of living a life. The voice haunts him, suggests there is a way. The argument of the poem continues: "He was old he is not real nothing is real/ Nor the noise of death drawing water" Merwin first denies the man because of his age, then denies his reality, then denies the reality of anything, distrusting even what he experiences, which resonates with the death of the man through his senses, the mouth, the eyes. The man cannot trust his sight, which is gone, and has only a song, an approximation of memory. Merwin has only his dreams, which he then dismisses as well. In his frustration, he distrusts everything.

Then, in typical Merwin paradox, he declares, "We are the echo of the future", a statement which implies that the future would have happened, otherwise there could be no echo. And an echo is something created by a prior utterance, and is lessened, often, in amplitude and clarity. The paradoxical inference, then, is that the future is what is real because it is what we imagine, what we seek, and what we pursue, and knowing the present makes the future less. Merwin postulates that our anticipation of it and our attempt to order it constitute the only reality. In this way, he is similar to poet Wallace Stevens, in that Stevens believed that the work of the imagination is the supreme human achievement and the only true reality.

Lofty as the notion is, Merwin differs from Stevens, as shown in the concluding stanza of the poem. However real or unreal the future is, he still seeks ways to live. He looks to the door, to a set of instructions which Jarold Ramsey suggests might even be Civil Defense instructions for what to do in the event of an atomic attack. It could just as easily be fire evacuation instructions, or any other disembodied, official set of orders, blandly noting what to do. As he reads the instructions, he realizes, "we were not born to survive/ Only to live"—a statement which implies that we live and accept our fate. To survive implies struggle, to overcome something, even if it's only finding a reason to endure.

"The River of Bees"

JAROLD RAMSEY ON MERWIN'S SEARCH FOR THE SELF'S LOST INTEGRITY

[Jarold Ramsey is Emeritus Professor of English at the University of Rochester. His research interests focus on American Indian literature, Shakespeare, and modern poetry. He is the author of the poetry collections, *The Space between Us*, *Love in an Earthquake*, *Dermographia*, and *Hand-Shadows*, as well as the editor and compiler of *Coyote Was Going There: Indian Literature of the Oregon Country* and *The Stories We Tell: An Anthology of Oregon Folk Literature* (with Suzi Jones). He has published numerous articles on Shakespeare, modern poetry, American Indian literature, and narrative theory. In the excerpt from his essay, "The Continuities of W.S. Merwin: 'What Has Escaped We Bring With Us,'" the critic writes that the poem reflects a struggle to understand identity and integrity.]

Is there, within the great indifferent Heraclitean strife and flow among things (itself threatened apocalyptically in our age) the possibility of a human order, a stable scheme of things caught and kept alive in the flux, not "lice" but the real and abiding terms of one's identity?

To return to the opening poem, "The Animals": in terms of the poet's quest for identity, for an integrity of being, those unseen, un-returning animals he is "remembering to invent names for"—are they not analogous to the "lice" of which his self seems chiefly to be composed? In "Is That What You Are," the title's question, ostensibly directed to a "New ghost ... / Standing on the stairs of water," recoils upon the speaker himself, as he wonders, the baffled quick confronting the enigmatic dead, "What failure still keeps you / Among us the unfinished" (*L*, 4).

The confrontation continues in that weirdly fine monologue, "The Hydra." Of all the poems in *The Lice*, it seems most truly to follow the first prediscursive stirrings of the mind, as if the poet were beginning to brood upon some ultimate riddle. Once sturdily possessed of the distinction between the living and the dead, the speaker admits that he now forgets "where the difference falls"; yet against the hydra song of Death, which "calls me Everybody," he tries to assert that "I know my name and do not answer." Against his half-envious view of the dead with their finalized identities and their freedom from "hesitations," having just confessed that he has forgotten the difference between them and himself, he characteristically contradicts himself and distinguishes life in the Heraclitean flow in these strange deathly terms:

> One thing about the living sometimes a piece of us
> Can stop dying for a moment
>
> (*L*, 5)

Are those transcendent moments what we are? Or are we rather the "lice" we bring with us?

Later in this book, in "The Plaster," Merwin describes how for him the house of an untimely dead writer is haunted by the poems he or she did not live to write. In the context I am trying to define, the meditation turns back upon its author, as in "Is That What You Are"; the last lines seem to return him to the identity half-hidden in his own incomplete career, with its burden of "lice"; "What is like you now / Who were haunted all your life by the best of you / Hiding in your death" (*L*, 40).

Glossing "The Lost Son," Theodore Roethke wrote that in that poem and throughout the middle of his career he proceeded from a belief that "to go forward as a spiritual man it is necessary first to go back," that is, through his own life.[11] But Merwin, in searching for the self's lost integrity, will not follow this program of progress-by-reversion. In one of the most personal poems in *The Lice*, "The River of Bees," the speaker in a dream recalls a Homeric blind old man seen fifteen years before who stood in the courtyard of a house beside a river and sang "of what was older." Rather like "Hydra," the poem evolves in terms of a vacillation between such affirmative and hopeful private memories of "what is older" and the general unreality and purposelessness of the present. It would be simpler, the poet might at least consolidate his despair, if he could forget the old singer, who, after all, must now be dead, obliterated—and anyway, in Heraclitean logic, is it not futile to return to the rivers of the past? But, in sequences like the following, something compels him to return in pain to a once open and *possible* life; having declared with a kind of bitter exultation against all humanistic aspiration, "Men think they are better than grass," in the next line he comes back wistfully to a time when the distinction seemed unimportant—

I return to his voice rising like a forkful of hay

but then the nullity of the present obscures that voice—

He was old he is not real nothing is real
Nor the noise of death drawing water

Harried by this fearful intuition, driven to wonder if "We are the echo of the future," he goes on asking, How shall I live? and as an artist, What shall I say? And in the crucible of this great poem, the poet achieves a brilliant fusion, at once plaintive and authoritative, of his private lostness and the lostness of an entire age, with its Civil Defense guides to postnuclear survival that no one really believes in—

On the door it says what to do to survive
But we were not born to survive
Only to live

(*L*, 32–33)

"How shall we live" in an age that is only the echo of its awful future? How can the song of the old blind goatherd teach us

---

now? It is in such poems as this one (and "The Widow," which follows it), achieving a terrible consonance of personal and public necessity, that Merwin has truly seized, in Laurence Lieberman's praise, "the peculiar spiritual agony of our time, and the agony of a generation which knows itself to be the last, and has transformed that agony into great art."[12]

NOTES

11. Theodore Roethke, *On the Poet and His Craft*, p. 39.
12. Laurence Lieberman, "Recent Poetry in Review," *Yale Review*, 57 (Summer 1968), 597.

> —Jarold Ramsey, "The Continuities of W.S. Merwin: 'What Has Escaped We Bring With Us.'" *W.S. Merwin: Essays on the Poetry*, Cary Nelson and Ed Folsom, eds. (Urbana: University of Illinois Press, 1987): pp. 38–40.

EDWARD J. BRUNNER ON THE POEM AS ELEGY

[In a description of three elegies in *The Lice*, Brunner here outlines how the poem is a distinct example of the form.]

"The Widow" is one of three elegies that question the survival of the human species. In "The Gods" it is

> the fighting in the valley
> The blows falling as rice and
> With what cause
> After these centuries gone (L, 30)

that lead him to doubt the species will continue: "What is man that he should be infinite." But the second elegy, "The River of Bees," is just different enough to count; in it, the memory of a house by a courtyard in which a blind man "stood singing / Of what was older" pains Merwin because it emphasizes his own remoteness from recollections of mysterious perfection: "I took my eyes / A long way to the calendars / Room after room asking how shall I live" (L, 32). Although he would identify with the blind man, urging himself to live, the best he can produce is: "Once once and once / In the same city I was born / Asking what shall I say." The blind man, who has somehow overcome his own grief and found contact with "what was older," stands apart, while Merwin knows only his own misery.

Yet Merwin's despair is not complete, even at this point in his volume. Lines twist and the poem shifts: "Men think they are better than grass // I return to his voice rising like a forkful of hay." Two voices contend for Merwin's allegiance in these two lines. The prophet's voice of the first line is dismissive and disdainful, castigating humans for their unforgivable arrogance, suggesting it is appropriate they cannot transcend their condition. But the voice of the second line, which hears the blind man's singing, chastens the first. It recalls that we can rise above our misery, that we do not pass away like numberless blades but inexplicably endure, that we can transcend our condition. This thought, however, is a torment, not a solace, because it poses an essential contrast: "But we were not born to survive / Only to live." To live, one would need to be like the blind man capable of singing; to survive is a lesser ambition, leading to the mistaken belief that "nothing is real," which virtually guarantees that humans will not survive.

The confusion and despair and misery here arise from Merwin's struggle to believe that the species is worthy of consideration. Worksheets for "April" show it began with doubts about a future in which the poet's words will matter. In one passage he conceives his present voice heard by us as emerging from the past. But then he mocks the idea that there can be any connection between the two:

Days to come
In which no stars are hidden

Who will know anything

Here in the past let us pretend

In a further draft, this last stanza sputters out: "Let us pretend there will be / Someone let us." Additional stanzas turn bitter: "A tongue is knowledge of its teeth / Full of sadness and without authority." But from all these options, Merwin shaped this final poem:

> When we have gone the stone will stop singing
>
> April April
> Sinks through the sand of names
>
> Days to come
> With no stars hidden in them
>
> You that can wait being there You that lose nothing
> Know nothing (L, 29)

From what has become the past, Merwin speaks to us in our present, his future. What we have no knowledge of, we cannot lose; if we never know the hidden stars, we can never miss them, and so we appear to Merwin as knowing nothing. But the new addition absent from worksheets is the opening line that focuses on Merwin in his present. The stones will stop singing, and the lovely name of "April April" will sink down through the endless sand of names and be lost—if those like Merwin, in the present that will be our past, fail to write of the hidden stars or the names like April. While the poem remains suffused with despair, what has been added is Merwin's own edge of responsibility, his impetus to transmit his immediate recognitions to us. The worksheets, that is, are dominated by the voice of despair, which says, "Men think they are better than grass," and prophesies doom; but the poem is animated when the second voice contends with the first by recalling the singing and passing it on, though such a feat may be useless. Even in this elegiac section, then, Merwin is alluding to some form of necessary action, some purifying change, that he would move toward despite its unlikelihood.

—Edward J. Brunner, *Poetry as Labor and Privelege: The Writings of W.S. Merwin* (Urbana: University of Illinois Press, 1991): pp. 142–143.

H.L. Hix on Merwin's Rejection of Natural Hierarchy

[In this excerpt, Hix puts the poem in the context of others from the poet's middle period, arguing that Merwin's work of that time rejects notions of human species superiority.]

When the narrator in W.S. Merwin's "The River of Bees" says—with evident sarcasm—that "Men think they are better than grass," he takes issue with a long tradition in western intellectual history of hierarchizing natural forms. Whether manifest as Heraclitus's contention that "the most beautiful of apes is ugly in comparison to the race of men, the wisest of men seems an ape in comparison to a god," or as Descartes' argument that animals not only "have less reason than men, but that they have none at all," or even as the hostile early response to Darwin's theory, the long-standard view has placed humans above the rest of nature. Merwin's dispute with the traditional view is not confined to "The River of Bees," but plays an important role in a sizeable portion of his work.

Merwin's corpus to date divides itself easily into three periods: an early period that runs through the first four books and ends abruptly at *The Moving Target*, with its use of "open form" in place of traditional metrical and stanzaic forms; a middle, oracular period that ends with *The Compass Flower*; and a late period of more transparently personal and intimate poetry, foretold by the anomalous *Finding the Islands* and then begun in earnest with the family poems in *Opening the Hand*.

Among its other distinctive features, the middle period is notable for its animism and primitivism. Merwin regularly treats inanimate objects (stones, crosses, dust, and so on) as if they were animate, and treats animals as if they were human. Within that broad pattern, there is a more particular pattern that leads to a kind of poem, the poem of abstraction's command, that can be read as the quintessence of Merwin's middle period. The more particular pattern is a thematic continuum that funnels from apostrophizing animals to apostrophizing abstraction(s), and culminates in reverse apostrophe, when the abstraction is heard addressing us.

In his early and late periods, Merwin shows no less interest in animals than in his middle period, but he maintains a different stance toward them. In the early and late periods, the distinction between humans and other animals remains intact, in the manner of Auden's "Their Lonely Betters": "As I listened from a beach-chair in the shade / To all the noises that my garden made, / It seemed to me only proper that words / Should be withheld from vegetables and birds."

In "Herons," for example, which takes its place in *A Mask for Janus* as the first poem in Merwin's collected work with the name of an animal in its title, the three herons—reminiscent of the three women in Yeats' "Friends"—seem to speak, but they do so only in a dream, the human narrator's dream, where their words clearly represent the words of the narrator or his unconscious. The herons have voice only insofar as they have been transported by the dream from their world into the narrator's. Similarly, in *The Dancing Bears*, the heron in "The Lady with the Heron" serves only as a correlative for the lady. The narrator's interest in the heron depends wholly on his interest in the lady, and he attributes to the heron no character or identity except as a figure for the lady.

Merwin's preoccupation with animals becomes the focal point of *Green with Beasts*, as the book's title indicates, but even so only the human voice has the authority to speak of and to the animals. The book's first part, "Physiologus: Chapters for a Bestiary," consists of a series in which each poem describes some animal or pair of animals. In each case, a human voice speaks about the animal from a point of view outside—and above—it. "This is the black sea-brute bulling through wave-wrack," the human narrator of the first poem, "Leviathan," begins. The narrator in

"Blue Cockerel" looks at "this bird" balancing, "His blue feet splayed." "White Goat, White Ram" gives a premonition of the coming change in point of view when the speaker recognizes how ironic it is that "out of our dumbness / We would speak for them, give speech to the mute tongues / Of angels," but the animals still remain a "them" apart from "us" throughout *Green with Beasts*, including the animal poems scattered through the rest of the book: "Burning the Cat," "Dog Dreaming," "A Sparrow Sheltering Under a Column of the British Museum," and others. The same stance defines the (far less frequent) animal poems in *The Drunk in the Furnace*, poems such as "Some Winter Sparrows."

In *The Moving Target*, though, the formal transition away from metrical forms and punctuation signals changes in voice, point of view, and theme, none more significant than the new way in which animals assert themselves in the poems. As early as the book's third poem, "Lemuel's Blessing," animals become subjects instead of objects. Though the poem begins with a human voice blessing a wolf distinct from itself ("I bless your paws and their twenty nails which tell their own prayer"), soon the identification with the wolf becomes so thorough that the subject and object are hard to distinguish. From a wish ("Let me wear the opprobrium of possessed and possessors / As a thick tail ...") the identification becomes a fact ("Deliver me / ... From the ruth of known paths, which would use my feet, tail, and ears as curios"). That identification paves the way for poems such as "Noah's Raven," in which the animal in the poem speaks for itself.

—H.L. Hix, "'A Simple Test': A Thematic Continuum in W.S. Merwin's Middle Period." *Many Mountains Moving* 4:2 (2002): pp. 68–69.

CRITICAL ANALYSIS OF
"The Asians Dying"

William H. Rueckert called "The Asians Dying" Merwin's most "explicit anti-Vietnam [sic] War poem." It was penned in 1967 at the height of the Vietnam War, and contains in it disturbing images of the dead of both sides, though their markedly different treatment by the poet (see Brunner, below) amplifies the poem's message.

The poem opens with an easily decipherable paradox: "When the forests have been destroyed their darkness remains". Darkness, here, carries its usual negative weight: foreboding, shadowy, menacing, and the like. Even though the trees have been defoliated, blasted, shot down, and sawed down, the darkness and threat is still present. But it is not the darkness and threat of possible peril; rather, it is the shadow of what happened. "The ash the great walker follows the possessors/ Forever", where the "great walker" can be considered the occupying power, or the United States military—as it follows the possessors, which could be read as soldiers. The "ash" is left in the wake of "possessors" sent on by the "great walker".

The terms "possessors" and "great walker" do not demonize individual soldiers. "Possessors" is a word more fraught with violation than occupiers, soldiers, or any similar official-ese. But by making the actors personified by their action rather than their military designation, the potential meaning of the word is simultaneously expanded and more pointed. As well, it compounds the sense of impersonality inherent in "great walker". The absence of corporeal forms of the "great walker" suggests a more ideological character, a composite of American governmental figures, MacNamara, Johnson, and so on. Their effect, their trailing ash, is permanent, is a "Forever", a designation so important as to merit an entire line devoted to its energy. The only other word to receive such treatment in this poem is, tellingly, "Remains". "Forever" extends the effect of the "possessors" will have on the spaces they have destroyed, or covered in ash.

As the "possessors" and "great walker" proceed, Merwin writes that "Nothing they will come to is real", and while it sounds at first like a typical Merwin utterance doubting the veracity of all outside of imagination, the meaning here is also more conventional when considered with the following line: "Nor for long". Thus, anything existing, will not for long.

The next image, one of migration, tells us the fate of the settlements of the Asians: "Over the watercourses/ Like ducks in the time of the ducks/ The ghosts of the villages trail in the sky/ Making a new twilight". The villages are now "ghosts" of ash and smoke, burned, the evidence of the fire darkening the sky, yielding a "new twilight". But the inclusion of the ducks implies, as Nelson points out, migration, movement, relocation. In the context of the poem, it is likely not a "good" relocation. Rather, the migration is to, perhaps, another plane, or another place of ash, a settling. The ghosts hover over water, ubiquitous in Vietnam, and so hover over a land on which it is difficult to settle.

The next image suggests the fate of the corporeal, in a less surreal and ghostly sense: "Rain falls into the open eyes of the dead/ Again again with its pointless sound/ When the moon finds them they are the color of everything". The image of the rain falling on the eyes of the dead, as Perloff and Nelson each point out, is striking, surprising, but logical and familiar at once. The lines are set into their own stanza, a raw presentation heightening the horror of the scene. The Asians are rendered real and mystical at once; that they are the "color of everything" is both a counterintuitive statement, even a nonsensical one, and one that, in the context of the scene, makes literal sense. Moonlight renders things a similar hue, as does decay and the settling of ash. There is the metaphorical sense that they have been changed to the common pallor of death or of the earth, as well. And there is the symbolic sense of their sameness in color as commented upon in the excerpts which follow. At the same time, the rain falls, unrelenting in its "Again again" and, Merwin tells us, "pointless" with its sound. Because it is pointless, it is thus unmoved by that which it rains on. The resonance of "pointless" also goes to the heart of the poet's feelings on the war, and its striking position in a line of familiar words gives it a prominence that underscores the prevailing sentiment.

Time passes. The night gives way: "The nights disappear like bruises but nothing is healed". The night, compared to a bruise, is thus a remnant of violence, and like a bruise, it fades, receding in pain and into the body. In this case, however, "nothing is healed". The next line treats the dead the same way, as bruises, fading (or, quite literally, sinking and decomposing), and thus unhealed. "The blood vanishes into poisoned farmlands" makes it clear that the lands were poisoned long before they were blood-fouled. Readers also realize the long term, unhealing damage wrought on the land, realizing that any future farming will be in the blood of the dead.

"Pain the horizon/ Remains/ Overhead the seasons rock" contains a variety of possible readings due to the absence of punctuation. The first two lines could be simple subject object inversion, meaning the horizon *remains* pain. A variant reading supports it, as the line literally reads as if an "is" is implied in the sentence: "Pain [is] the horizon," making pain both an image of the horizon and a fact of eventuality; the horizons for the Asians are simply more pain. By placing "Remains" on its own line, Merwin reiterates the presence of the dead, whether the word is linked to the other lines or not. "Overhead the seasons rock" could be the start of a new idea or part of the preceding two lines, that the horizon, if it *is* pain, is still "overhead". Either way, the "seasons rock/ They are paper bells/ Calling to nothing living". The paper bells call to mind notions of flimsiness, as well as the American kitschy item, the "Chinese lantern," and Western stereotypes of Asians. They are unheard, both as paper and because no one is present to hear their call. The dead do not answer for these bells tolling to them, to these seasons passing. The entire stanza intimates that time passes but death remains, and that the land is ruined, to the horizon, and that the few noises which remain call to nothing. The hurt and violation is permanent.

The only thing which continues is the "possessors" who, in

the next stanza, are continuing. They "move everywhere under Death their star". Like the Asians, they too are ensnared in Death, but in a far more abstract relationship than that of rain drops falling on open eyes. Death is so distant that it is a star, but its light (or lack, see below) is always on them. "Like columns of smoke they advance into the shadows". They are insubstantial, the manifest of ruin, smoke. They are the after effect of burning, and they advance into a darkness deeper than that made by their columns. They are "Like thin flames with no light", so destructive that they burn without shedding light. The similarities between lightless fire and a star of death resonate in the final stanza, just as villages migrate in smoke, making a new, lightless twilight.

Finally, the possessors are "They with no past/ And fire their only future". They move from destruction, obliterating any past, any sense of the violation they have committed (as they are free from knowing the burden of their history), and move on to the lightless burning that unites the imagery of the final stanza. This ending is like so many of Merwin's, which Stephen Dunn characterized as ending with possibility, and not an end *per se*. The awful possibility at the end of "The Asians Dying" is that the destruction is perpetual, constantly in the present, and open and brutal and permanent.

"The Asians Dying"

JAN B. GORDON ON RUIN

[Jan B. Gordon is the author of *Gossip and Subversion in Nineteenth-Century Novel: Echo's Economies*, as well as articles on literature and medicine, nineteenth-century literature, and contemporary Asian poetry. He is on the faculty of Tokyo University of Foreign Studies. Gordon considers Merwin's approaches to writing the void, the central concern of much of the poet's work through his so-called middle period. In the excerpt, Gordon draws a distinction between concepts of ruin and ruins, or relics, themselves.]

The ruin is to the history of civilization as a mythology of origins is to a highly self-conscious work of art. The historian may regard Robert Louis Stevenson's account of the circumstances surrounding the authorship of *Dr. Jekyll and Mr. Hyde* as being literally true, whereas the critic recognizes that such is a part of intentionality. The myth of its origins is not part of the story's history, but part of its art; it is art using history as a mask in the effort to reconstitute its "origins" which it can only fictionalize as a "beginning." Such "stories" most often accompany Gothic or grotesque works like those of Poe and Coleridge, and represent history struggling with itself. It is not only that the Gothic contains the "hidden" aspects of our past in its abandoned cathedrals and tombs, but that in its structure it attempts a *recovery* in a double sense. On the emotional and psychic level, the unconscious approaches the condition of the ruin: it is part of our collective heritage; it consists of fragments of past experiences and wishes; and it is the foundation of civilization. It differs from its architectonic counterpart primarily in the accessibility of its parts. It is not a genuine *mystery*, but a *mystification*, and *recovery* is less at stake than simple *retrieval*.

Merwin's poems often depend upon a confusion between

these two types of ruins, so that surrealism and surrealistic images merge with relics to produce something that approaches allegory at one limit and a personal cosmology at another. As opposed to the retrieval that goes on in a poem like "In the Winter of My Thirty-Eighth Year," there is the genuine recovery of those openly political poems, "The Asians Dying" and "When the War Is Over." The Asians, unlike all of the others in *The Lice* who must find some way of coming to terms with the dichotomy that separates personal and cosmic history, have no past. They carry the bones of dead relatives and the empty accoutrements of their presence. To them, building is synonymous with dwelling:

When the forests have been destroyed their darkness remains
The ash the great walker follows the possessors
Forever
Nothing they will come to is real
Not for long
Over the watercourses
Like ducks in the time of ducks
The ghosts of the villages trail in the sky
Making a new twilight

("The Asians Dying")

Their history is the year of the duck, not a museum containing its stuffed body. The line "Like ducks in the time of ducks" is the revelation of a vanishing for which Merwin has been looking throughout the volume:

Having crowded once onto the threshold of morality
And not been chosen
There is no freedom such as theirs
That have no beginning

The air itself is their memory
A domain they cannot inhabit
But from which they are never absent

("Divinities")

Such figures contain their own incompleteness. Never to inhabit is also never to undergo the terror of departure. Both "The Asians Dying" and "Divinities" are, thematically and structurally, odes, but by abandoning the customary preposition of address, "to," the speaker depletes them of their objectness and hence removes them as a locus of attachment for mnemosyne. There are seldom any possessives in the grammar of *The Lice*; he rather works within the logic of the predicate adjective which tends to reduce all to identities in a different conspiracy. He truly looks for the spirit that "follows the possessors / Forever." The Asians and the Divinities live amidst their own ruin and do not have a sense of history, but *are* history.

—Jan B. Gordon, "The Dwelling of Disappearance: *W.S. Merwin's The Lice.*" *Modern Poetry Studies* 3:3 (1972): pp. 135–136.

L. EDWIN FOLSOM ON IMPLICIT IMPERIALISM

[L. Edwin Folsom is Carver Professor of English at the University of Iowa and is a leading Whitman scholar. He is the author or editor of six books on Whitman, including *Whitman East and West: New Contexts for Reading Walt Whitman*, as well as two works about Merwin: *W.S. Merwin: Essays on the Poetry* and *Regions of Memory: Uncollected Prose of W. S. Merwin*, both co-edited with Cary Nelson. The piece is taken from a longer essay comparing Merwin's obsession with the meaning of America to Walt Whitman's. In particular, he looks at the imperialistic urge Merwin portrays in "The Asians Dying."]

This poem, says Harvey Gross, "dramatizes nature's revenge against men...." ... But it is not nature gaining her revenge so much as nature's *shadow*—a hollow, dark force of non-nature, of obliterated nature, a dark, non-palpable reminder of what used to be. It is the *lack* of nature that creeps back over the continent, obliterating man. It is the *exhaustion* of natural resources that causes the machines to cease functioning and leads man back to a primitive state, forced once again to use sticks and his hands, because there is no energy left for his machines. As so often in *The Lice*, Merwin here personifies emptiness or nothing; the Nothing of destroyed nature is what will kill man, finally; Americans think they have conquered the wilderness, only to find that No-Wilderness will conquer them. This poem demonstrates the anti-creation of America; the movement here is from west to east as the poem of America is erased, the creation of America wiped out, and nothing is left, finally, but barren, empty, lifeless land. The virgin She was destroyed, and now her destroyer, the American He, is likewise demolished. Nothing remains. There is no sense of hope further West in the Far East (no "Passage to India" as there was for the later Whitman); the only (faint) hope is in the few chastened men who escape with their shadows, left to gnaw the crust of the earth in some remote corner of the ruined country.

Later in *The Lice*, Merwin looks at America's continued attempts to expand westward by going to Viet Nam. In *"Asians Dying,"* the same process of de-creation is described as Americans destroy another wilderness further West in the Far East.... Even if Americans seek to complete Columbus' original goal to voyage to the Far East, suggests Merwin, they will only lay it to waste, too. The frontier, for Merwin, seems to be the meeting point not of "savagery and civilization" (as [Frederick Jackson] Turner defined it), but of pure nature and ash, the great walker. (pp. 63–4)

Throughout *The Lice*, Merwin's soul tries to fly, to transcend, to surge ahead like a Whitmanian soul, but the future is dead now; we are preparing *"For a Coming Extinction,"* ... and so Whitman's spirit is gone—"The tall spirit who lodged here has / Left already"—and the spirit of the new poet is wingless; it cannot fly or transcend; there is no future to soar into, nothing to expand into and name.... (pp. 64–5)

The self in these poems is infested with lice, with diseased things it cannot find and kill and so must carry with it. Whitman's self sought to contain all, to embody past, present, and future; Merwin's self seeks to contain nothing, to empty itself of a dead past ..., a shattered present, and a dead and destructive future.... Memory is no virtue for Merwin, for he seeks to break off from a meaningless past.... Not to repossess the past, then, is to be in total darkness, but at least free; the need here—and it is opposite the need of Whitman—is to *empty* the self, to find a new void within, and then to listen and learn from the silence of a de-created history: "Now all my teachers are dead except silence." ... (pp. 65–6)

[With Merwin's anti-song, the] American self/poem/country has ended its expansion and has entered its inevitable diminishment. The signs are on the pages themselves: Whitman's poems expand and flow, filling the void of the blank page with seemingly endless sentences; Merwin's poems, in stark contrast, are fragments, remnants: short, quiet markings that leave most of the page unfilled; the gaping void is creeping back in, threatening the very existence of speech. It is not a creative void that Merwin faces, not something he expands into and absorbs; rather, it is a destructive void which opens its dark abyss, ready to swallow the poet and all of life with him. It is the anti-creation of America, and the American poet—in contrast to his earlier, arrogant stance— retreats in quiet terror. "*Song of Myself*" ends confidently, sure of the self, looking outward toward ever-expanding journeys even in death: "If you want me again look for me under your boot-soles.... / Missing me one place search another, / I stop somewhere waiting for you." *The Lice* ends in a muted echo of these last words, with the Merwin-self divided, unsure, tentative: "Where else am I walking even now / Looking for me." ... (p. 66)

—L. Edwin Folsom, "Approaches and Removals: W. S. Merwin's Encounter with Whitman's America." *Shenandoah* (Spring 1978): pp. 63–64.

Marjorie Perloff on Strangeness and Clarity in Merwin's Work

[In this excerpt, taken from a longer essay about sorrow in Merwin's poems, she shows how his layers of meaning contribute to complex notions of sadness and loss.]

"For the Anniversary of My Death" is thus a very elegant, well-made poem; it has a finish that would be the envy of any number of poets, and its theme is certainly universal—just mysterious enough to arrest the reader's attention, yet just natural enough (this is the way we all feel about death sometimes) to have broad appeal. It is, I think, this blend of strangeness and a clear-sighted literalness that makes a poem like "The Asians Dying" memorable. Consider the lines

> Rain falls into the open eyes of the dead
> Again again with its pointless sound
> When the moon finds them they are the color of everything
>
> (L, 63)

We don't usually think of rain falling precisely into open eyes, let alone "the open eyes of the dead." The image is an odd one and yet the third line has a kind of photographic accuracy: in the moonlight, the dead bodies, clothed in khaki, would indeed blend with the colors of the forest ground, and so theirs is "the color of everything." Add to this the irony—a rather heavy-handed irony, I think—of Merwin's implication that, in our world, the color of death has become "everything," and you have an intricate enough layering of meanings, which is not to say that Merwin's construction is in any way radical or subversive. Indeed, I submit that nothing in "The Asians Dying" has the startling modernity of

> I was neither at the hot gates
> Nor fought in the warm rain
> Nor knee deep in the salt marsh, heaving a cutlass,
> Bitten by flies, fought.

Cary Nelson has rightly noted Merwin's debt to Eliot (p. 119), but it is a good question whether "Gerontion" doesn't capture what Lieberman calls "the peculiar spiritual agony of our time" at least as well as do poems like "The Asians Dying."

—Marjorie Perloff, "Merwin and the Sorrows of Literary History." *W.S. Merwin: Essays on the Poetry*, Cary Nelson and Ed Folsom, eds. (Urbana: University of Illinois Press, 1987): pp. 136–137.

WILLIAM H. RUECKERT ON MERWIN'S POLITICAL POEMS

[William H. Rueckert is known as the "dean of Kenneth Burke scholars." His books include *Critical Responses to Kenneth Burke: 1924–1966*, *Kenneth Burke and the Drama of Human Relations*, and *Encounters with Kenneth Burke*. In 2002, Parlor Press published *Letters from Kenneth Burke to William H. Rueckert, 1959–1987*. Rueckert also coined the term "ecocriticism," and is regarded as one of its foremost practitioners. He is Emeritus Professor of English at SUNY Geneseo. In an essay considering *The Lice* and its sources, Rueckert considers the political convictions behind a number of the poems in the collections, and the excerpt deals specifically with "The Asians Dying" and the two political poems immediately following it.]

Anyone who has heard Merwin read and talked with him knows that he has both an acute political and an ecological consciousness. In fact, the two are not really separable and in some ways all of the ecological poems in *The Lice* are also political. They certainly express a particular kind of individual response to the political realities of our time, a feeling of helplessness, despair, and shame. "Unfinished Book of Kings" is about a massive failure of the kind of vision which would make a new political leadership possible. The prophets are all dead and at the end of the poem we have the king of absences crowned. Perhaps this "Book of Kings" is unfinished because there are no more kings to write about, there is no one who will lead us out of bondage and there are no more prophets who can provide the vision necessary to guide us—the nation—toward a better life.

Three political poems in a row occur on pages 63–68 of *The Lice*: "The Asians Dying," "When the War Is Over," and "Peasant." "When the War Is Over" is one of the most straightforward poems in the book. It is obviously political and ironic and needs no analysis. It belongs to a small group of poems in the book which do not require critical mediation. "The Asians Dying" is Merwin's most explicit anti-Vietnam War poem. Though the poem is neither overtly political nor anti-American, no American reader who lived through that time would need to have the poem's powerful self-accusing political thrust explained. Though the poem mostly concentrates on effects rather than causes, those responsible are everywhere present and indicted in the poem as the "possessors." The "possessors" will be followed and haunted forever by the ghosts of their victims; "nothing they will come to" will be "real" again; the "possessors" have "Death" as "their star"; they become what they do: they have no past and only fire, or destruction, for their future.

"Peasant" is the most complex of these three poems. The subtitle indicates that the poem is the peasant's "Prayer to the Powers of This World," which makes it a kind of dramatic monologue addressed to the rulers and oppressors from the ruled and oppressed, to those with power from one who is powerless and helpless. A strong social consciousness is at work in the poem and makes us think of "Pieces for Other Lives" and, by association, poems such as "For a Coming Extinction," where a comparably strong ecological consciousness is at work. A strong ontological consciousness, of course, is everywhere present in the book.

The poem as prayer. A prayer is an approach to deity in word or thought; an earnest request; a form of entreating, imploring, supplicating; an address with adoration, confession, supplication, or thanksgiving (Webster). Kenneth Burke has said—in *The Philosophy of Literary Form*—that all poetry can be divided into the categories of dream, prayer, and chart. *The Lice* is full of dream poems. By "chart," Burke says he means poems that realistically size up situations, even if they do not always tell us what to do about them. But the poem as prayer. How many other prayers are there in *The Lice*: who or what is there to pray to? The Widow does not hear you and "your cries are numberless." "Peasant" is all irony, or prayer-canceling; it is an indictment of the powers of this world in the form of an ironic prayer to them. It is more chart than prayer when one is done with it and sizes up both the situation of the oppressed and the nature and character of the oppressors. The one authentic prayer in this book is Necessity (Nature?). It is not till *The Carrier of Ladders* that Merwin is able to write prayers, since prayers do have to be addressed to someone or something. *The Lice* is a book of dreams and charts.

—William H. Rueckert, "Rereading The Lice." *W.S. Merwin: Essays on the Poetry*, Cary Nelson and Ed Folsom, eds. (Urbana: University of Illinois Press, 1987): pp. 62–64.

Cary Nelson on the Poem's Echoes

[Nelson's excerpt is taken from a longer essay in which Nelson considers how Merwin's layered abstractions deconstruct ideas and specific histories. In the portion excerpted, he considers the ways in which "The Asians Dying" decays as readers "possess" it and become, in the language of the poem, "possessors."]

Merwin's "The Asians Dying" is his most famous poem overtly about the Vietnam War; it merits an analysis by infiltration, a criticism surrounded and deadened by the poem's political echoes. I quote the poem's lines, in order, interspersed with my commentary. "When the forests have been destroyed," he writes, "their darkness remains," their heaviness and their thick foliage weigh on us like our guilt. No defoliation, no consuming fire, is decisive. The landscape, leveled in the outside world, rises again in us. The shadows amongst the trees are now a brooding absence and an inner darkness. In our eyes are traces of each obliteration; our will is choked by compulsion, our sight layered with erasures:

The ash the great walker follows the possessors
Forever
Nothing they will come to is real
Nor for long

As readers, we too are possessors, but the poem's images *decay* through association. The enlightenment the poem offers is experienced, paradoxically, as suffocation. We are possessed by a past which invades each anticipation; ruinous memories seep into every future.

> —Cary Nelson, "Merwin's Deconstructive Career." In *W.S. Merwin: Essays on the Poetry*, Cary Nelson and Ed Folsom, eds., (Urbana: University of Illinois Press, 1987): pp. 98–99, 104–105.

EDWARD J. BRUNNER ON DEATH AS A HUMAN LINK

[In this excerpt, Brunner points out that death is a common link between people of varying circumstances in Merwin's poems. In particular, Brunner considers the poems written at the same time as "The Asians Dying," but in the excerpt below, Brunner details the link of death between the Asians and the American soldiers, despite vastly different treatments by the poet.]

One difference between the opening set of poems written in New York in the winter of 1963 and this midpoint cluster written in France in 1964 and 1965 is that the wintriness of the opening set is a state of mind possessed by Merwin, while the cold of the later group is a physical condition that generates its surprising oppositions. An even more dramatic difference separates the two: real deaths are under consideration in the final group, while the only death acknowledged in the opening set is metaphorical.[8]

In the closing group, death is an occurrence that links us with others. This realistic acknowledgment of death can appear with the old abstract concept in the same poem; it is one reason why the ending of "The Asians Dying" is so powerful. In the middle of the poem, Merwin uses "the dead" to speak of persons who were once alive: "Rain falls into the open eyes of the dead / Again again with its pointless sound / When the moon finds them they are the color of everything" (L, 70). Their "open eyes" also proclaim their status as individuals, not generic categories. Like the animals who would "look carefully" and return the glance of the poet in "The Animals," perhaps even speaking back to him, these too would look back accusingly if they could. But at the end of the poem, the old abstract, categorical idea of death emerges again, as "the possessors moved everywhere under Death their star." For the possessors, death is as remote as a star, an emblem calling them forward in their rapacious progress; it is a concept, having nothing to do with individuals. The two versions of death radically distinguish Asians from Americans, a distinction underscored with irony: the death the Asians experience leaves them with their eyes open; the death star under which the possessors march leaves them as blind as ever.

NOTE

8. MS. 21:02/015, d. May 1, 1964.

—Edward J. Brunner, *Poetry as Labor and Privelege: The Writings of W.S. Merwin* (Urbana: University of Illinois Press, 1991): pp. 147–148.

CRITICAL ANALYSIS OF

"Departure's Girl-friend"

This poem, from Merwin's 1963 collection, *The Moving Target*, is told from the point of the view of a woman, ostensibly "Departure's Girl-friend," who goes to a wharf, to board, she thinks, her boat, but is rebuffed by a dock hand. His rebuff instantly returns her to the city where she was born, a place of rot which she despises, and where she walks, hoping for another departure from the place.

The poem's surreal imagery mixes with a plainspoken monologue, suggesting a multiplicity of possible readings (see Christhilf, below). At the same time, the assertions of competing realities lend to the voice an authority greater than what a more conventional narrator of such a tale might provide. This poem, written around 1961, carries, like "The Drunk in the Furnace," vestiges of Merwin's earlier, formal concerns. The lines mostly carry four stresses, and stanza breaks preserve the ...

The "Girl-friend" starts by saying, "Loneliness leapt in the mirrors, but all week/ I kept them covered like cages." The image, a metaphor for the suddenness with which she realized her emotional state, also has the narrator in a position of trying to control that which leaps at her. She covers the mirrors. As Brunner claims, the narrator uses the loneliness as an occasion to act, rather than wallow in the negative. She says, "Then I thought/ Of a better thing."

Despite the late hour, she goes, "on my way/ To my boat, feeling good to be going, hugging/ This big wreath with the words like real/ Silver: *Bon Voyage.*" Merwin's conspicuous break at "real/ Silver" underscores that the occasion is one invented by the narrator, is an emotional dealing with the loneliness at hand. The percussive sound of the 'g' in the lines lends purpose to the imagined stride here. Another unusual decision here is for her to make or obtain her own *Bon Voyage* wreath. The decision reminds the reader that no one will make the wreath for her. She is so alone, so desirous of flight, that she provides her own pomp for the circumstance.

She continues in the following stanza: "The night/ Was mine but everyone's, like a birthday./ Its fur touched my face in passing." Like loneliness, here the night is given a metaphorical treatment. The association with fur, of coats, of splendor (of a dated, mid-century pre-PETA variety) matches with the almost "real" silver and the wreath. She intends to welcome everyone, but again, no one else is present. When she says she is going down "to my boat, my boat," the repetition, we learn later, is to convince herself of its veracity. She has no boat, as is made plain to her in the fifth stanza.

The moment is made the more strange because she plans "To see it off," and she is "glad at the thought." If it is her boat, readers may ask, who will pilot it out on its voyage? To whom is she wishing a good journey? The sadness of what is to come emerges in the next several images. "Some leaves of the wreath were holding my hands/And the rest waved good-bye as I walked, as though/ They were still alive." We are reminded that the wreath, however joyous, is constructed of dead plants, and artificial silver, commemorating something which will not happen. The wreath holds her hand, and it seems she is denying, perhaps, how tightly she is, in fact, clinging to the wreath.

The devastation begins in the one-line fourth stanza: "And all went well till I came to the wharf, and no one." While she makes clear in the next stanza that, in point of fact, someone *is* decidedly *there*, he is not what she imagined. The "fur" of the night suggested some imagined society, some friends and well-wishers, perhaps those who envy her.

Instead, "There was this young man, maybe/ Out of the merchant marine," and her association of him with "no one" is exactly the association he will have for her, and which will upset her and break the spell, sending her back to the city. He is, she says, "In some uniform," identifying him immediately as a person of faceless and unparticular resistance to her. Even the rebuff is not by someone known, compounding the sense of isolation and loneliness that she suffers. However, that she says, "and I knew who he was" indicates that she has either tried the act before, or that she has at least spent enough time around wharves to know the functions of the uniformed men who walk their piers.

She does add, "just the same/ When he said to me where do you think you're going,/ I was happy to tell him." Her happiness implies either a sense that she mistakenly believes in her quest, or that she is happy to play the game. The resulting conversation, however, makes clear the level of her delusion. She tries to offer the wreath as proof of her ownership of a boat, and the uniformed man rudely dismisses her: "this is the stone wharf, lady,/ You don't own anything here."

She turns away, and the "injustice of it/ Lit up the buildings, and there I was/ In the other and hated city", a city we can assume is the one that was always there, but this one is unchanged by her imaginative projections. In other words, his reply brings her, more or less, down to earth. Even as it does, however, we realize her perception of it is still surreal to readers' perceptions. It is where she "was born," and the meaning could either be literal, or closer to the sense that her experiences in the city led to her present state of mind. Either way, the city is a place "where nothing is moored, where/ The lights crawl over the stone like flies, spelling now,/ Now," and the effect is one of a city unstable, like her, and vaguely menacing. The lights "crawl" in monstrous movements. The movements spell "now" twice, reminding her of the irrevocable present, that place she does not wish to inhabit, from which she wishes to depart. The title of the poem, in fact, suggests a devotion to departure, a love of leaving, a near betrothal to the idea.

For, in the end, she is tried of "the same fat chances" that "roll/ Their many eyes". Again, a monstrous image for the horror of possibility. In a place "unmoored," all chances are fat, full of potential, of change, of the various differences that threaten stability, something this narrator can scarcely cling to. As well, the meaning of "fat chance" (paradoxically) is the same as "slim chance," or somewhat hopeless, such that perhaps the fat options are all equally despairing. The city is a monstrous, consumptive, pitiless place of rejection of the imaginative soul she possesses.

Yet, amidst the uncertainty, she steps "once more/ Through a hoop of tears" and proceeds. She is doing it "once more", already familiar with this process of imagining something, dealing with the reality, and persisting. But she holds the fragile thing of her making in front of her, almost as a shield: "holding this/ Buoy of flowers in front of my beauty," and she is far more direct than the stylized faux-silver French phrase. She says she will wish herself "the good voyage."

"Departure's Girl-Friend"

KENNETH ANDERSEN ON MERWIN'S DEVELOPING CONCERN WITH MOTION

[At the time the article was written, Kenneth Andersen was at Columbia University. While Andersen describes, throughout the longer article, Merwin's poetry as one of a "distinct evolution," he singles out "Departure's Girl-friend," with other poems, as emblematic of Merwin's concern with motion: moving on, moving toward death, motion as struggle.]

There are a few poems in this volume which provide us with a more affirmative view of Merwin as a poet and as a man. In these poems, the redeeming factor is the sparse but precious conviction of self which he asserts in the modern age. Thus, in "Departure's Girl-Friend," the poet insists upon the integrity and validity of his journey in spite of the personal hazards and the common resistance to his course when he says,

>   and I step once more
> Through a hoop of tears and walk on, holding this
> Buoy of flowers in front of my beauty,
> Wishing myself the good voyage. (36)

And in the last poem of the book, "Daybreak," the artist does not revel either in his arrogance or in his despondency, but rather triumphantly and heroically re-asserts himself upon a future quest into the unknown:

> Again this procession of the speechless
> Bringing me their words
> The future woke me with its silence
> I join the procession

An open doorway
Speaks for me
Again. (97)

The Lice (New York, 1967), Merwin's latest book of poems, represents both a new departure and an old survival. New poetic elements in evidence are an absence of punctuation in the text, making the thought more open-minded and suggestive; an increasing versatility in a number of poetic forms; a maturing sense of the nuances of poetic metaphor and rhythm; and an artistic concern which now reaches occasionally into the public, as opposed to the private, sphere. Merwin's early poetry contributes other elements: a growing appreciation, once again, for poetic complexity, both in thought and in form; a muted, understated, and restlessly gentle style of writing, reminiscent of *The Dancing Bears* and *Green with Beasts*; a sympathetic understanding of the inexplicable ironies of life, recalling *The Drunk in the Furnace*; and perhaps a touch of lingering pessimism. *The Lice*, then, is a volume of poetry constructed upon a dialectic between the poetic lessons of the past and a healthy experimentation of the present. And it is out of this dialectic, or tension, between opposing influences that the beauty and animation of his poetry comes.

Curiously, the poems in this collection are almost wholly about the future and about death. The titles of the poems easily betray their ominous content: "Some Last Questions," "The Last One," "News Of the Assassin," "The Mourner," "For The Anniversary Of My Death," "The Asians Dying," "For A Coming Extinction," and "Death Of A Favorite Bird." The intensity and impact of these poems comes primarily from the last few lines of each verse, where the poet deftly manages to condense a thought, and then suddenly expand it far beyond the barriers of the poem itself: "... but you the dead / Once you go into those names you go on you never / Hesitate / You go on" ("The Hydra," 5); "... the names / Do not come down to us / On the way to them the words / Die" ("An End in Spring," 7); and lastly, "... that my words are the garment of what I shall never be

/ Like the tucked sleeve of a one-armed boy" ("When You Go Away," 62).

One cannot help feeling that "In The Winter of My Thirty-Eighth Year" (61), recalling Dylan Thomas, is one of Merwin's finer poems. The poet's persistent theme throughout this collection, the passage of life toward the future and toward death, is here given memorable, and enduring, form. The skill of the artist is evident in many ways: in the telescoping of the thoughts of the future coupled with the remembrance of youth; in the fluid but precise phrasing ("No older at all it seems from here / As far from myself as ever"); in the crisp and evocative images ("Walking in fog and rain and seeing nothing / I imagine all the clocks have died in the night"); and in an uncanny ability to suggest, through the nuances of rhythm and line, the inexorable movement of man toward death and, at the same time, the stillness of a moment of contemplative thought. All of these qualities are perhaps summed up best in the last stanza of the poem, a stanza which, through the image of the stars, catches perfectly the essential loneliness which the poet feels, midway between his birth and his death:

Of course there is nothing the matter with the stars
It is my emptiness among them
While they drift farther away in the invisible morning.

With his later poetry, then, especially with the poems collected in *The Lice*, W.S. Merwin has come of age as an artist. His development, significantly, has been distinguished by his definitions of, his views on, and the confrontation with those ultimate tragic questions which concern us all. As has been mentioned in the beginning, Merwin has created not only diverse works of art but also, within this art, a synthetic philosophy which depends, for its very foundation, on a vital, changing point of view. Thus in his poetry we pass from the personal sense of alienation as an artist ("What fable should I tell them, / That they should believe me?") in "When I came from Colchis," to the triumphant answer in the "All metaphor ... is magic" success of the resounding "Leviathan"; from the "mad precarious man / Making a prayer for folly" in the "Fable," to the quiet assurance of a perceptive artist giving "shapes to the sprawled sea" in "The Bones"; from the interwoven complexity of "Evening with Lee Shore and Cliffs," to the simplicity and innocence of his family portraits in *The Drunk in the Furnace*; and from an affirmation of the voyaging self in "Daybreak," to a recognition, in "In The Winter of My Thirty-Eighth Year," that both the self and the voyage are as elusive as the uncertain future.

—Kenneth Andersen. "The Poetry of W.S. Merwin." *Twentieth Century Literature* 16:4 (1970): pp. 284–285.

Mark Christhilf on the Artist's Struggle

[In a chapter that ultimately concludes that Merwin is a Romantic, Christhilf here considers how the poem carries a dual message: the story on its face, and its representation of the struggle of the creative artist in a world which neither makes a place for him nor cares.]

More vigorous forms of resistance are imagined in several of Merwin's poems. In "The Next" of *The Moving Target*, resistance is expressed as a bold and courageous protest against a conspiracy to deprive the people of their life and limb. Yet in this poem and elsewhere Merwin implies that protest will have little effect on the course of history. For this reason Merwin most often imagines resistance as an act of departure—as simple movement away from the reductive pressure of historical life. Echoing the mythical theme of exploration from Merwin's early poetry, the motif of departure reveals his inability to find justice in any sociohistorical mode of identity. In "Departure's Girl-Friend" he describes an event in which the speaker refuses the identity that society would unjustly impose. Attempting to escape her loneliness as the poem begins, she decides to take a voyage in her boat and walks through the city toward the wharf, carrying a wreath of flowers. At the wharf she encounters the representative of the sociohistorical moment. When he asks where she is going, she tells him with openness that she is going to her boat, and in his response Merwin typifies the society's unwillingness to understand her as she understands herself: "He said, this is the stone wharf, lady, / You don't own anything here." As she turns away and moves on, Merwin insists on the self's right to define itself over and beyond any social definition. "I step once more / Through a hoop of tears and walk on," she says, "holding this / Buoy of flowers in front of my beauty, / Wishing myself the good voyage."

"Departure's Girl-Friend" indicates a reason for the success of Merwin's story of humankind. A poem containing more than one level of meaning, it ultimately expresses Merwin's struggle to survive as a creative artist in the modern world that holds no inspiration for him. The poem discloses an effort to preserve imagination in "the other and hated city"—amid a landscape of technological objects and among a majority of human beings overwhelmingly unsympathetic to poetic imagination. In framing his own sense of rejection, Merwin appealed to a postwar generation that feared that a technological organization of life was the enemy of individuality. This generation came to be guided by the existentialist assumption that there is no justice in any social authority that denies the primacy of self-expression. In this respect the social encounters in Merwin's poetry tell an existentialist's tale.

Ultimately this view toward society is the Romantic one, placing Merwin's poetry in the American tradition of Thoreau and Samuel Clemens. In the tradition of radical innocence, the American Adam moves away from all social convention and prevailing belief. The question arising with regard to this tradition should be applied to Merwin's poetry: is there a "moving target" justifying flight from society? What source of solace outside the self is to be asserted? In a number of poems Merwin indicates as an objective a past mode of belief through which to redeem the present. There is elegiac yearning for this past from which historical man has fallen in Merwin's "Resolution," in *The Moving Target*. The speaker hears a child playing piano music that becomes less audible even as he is threatened by a vague coercive force. Apparently he feels that time is taking him away from inspiriting sources, for he declares near the end of the poem:

Oh let it be yesterday surely
It's time. (68)

—Mark Christhilf, *W.S. Merwin the Mythmaker* (Columbia: University of Missouri Press, 1986): pp. 28–30.

Edward J. Brunner on the Poem as a Breakthrough

[Brunner tracks the development of Merwin's so-called urban poems, and in this excerpt, describes how "Departure's Girl-friend" deserves more than ordinary attention because of its distinct purposefulness, and how that purposeful character was a breakthrough for Merwin's emerging style.]

"Departure's Girl-friend," the first of these consciously urban poems, is a breakthrough of considerable magnitude: though he begins his second cycle as he had his first, with a dramatic monologue spoken by another, the situation has markedly changed. The poem has a swiftness of purpose, an intent focus, missing from its predecessors. It begins with a purposive gesture; instead of avoiding loneliness by suppressing it, the speaker takes it as an occasion to act, and that decision transforms her surroundings, so that "The night / Was mine but everyone's, like a birthday." The "bon voyage" wreath she has concocted for delivery to her boat even feels responsive; its leaves were "holding my hands," and "the rest waved good-bye." But there is no delivery to be made, no boat at the wharf—and though the speaker insists that the wreath she hugs to herself grants her the right to expect her boat, the truth is delivered bluntly by a sailor: "He said, this is the stone wharf, lady, / You don't own anything here." But from this dismissal emerges a vision of the city in sharp focus:

> and there I was
> In the other and hated city
> Where I was born, where nothing is moored, where
> The lights crawl over the stones like flies, spelling now,
> Now, and the same fat chances roll
> Their many eyes; and I step once more
> Through a hoop of tears and walk on, holding this
> Buoy of flowers in front of my beauty,
> Wishing myself the good voyage. (MT, 36)

Those who would be so foolish, in the city, as to expect events to conform to their wishes will always be disappointed, for "nothing is moored," and the bottom continually drops out. But just as the city places the protagonist, the protagonist finds the strength to place the city. That "other and hated city" is by no means portrayed as devouring the speaker: its blazing lights are reduced to crawling flies, its opportunistic offerings to the "same fat chances." Understanding the city's energetic aimlessness, the speaker can now comprehend herself, in a way that is ironic yet not self-lacerating. The wry tone into which she falls is, in fact, her triumph. At the very end, she has the strength to see herself against the city, a new version of the mirror she had so conspicuously avoided at the start.

The urban backdrop is a fractured mirror, a testing-ground upon which one learns survival. It tests the wreaths one weaves around oneself like protective amulets; it may expose their inadequacy even as it reveals they are needed all the more. The wreath in which the speaker invested so much, which hovered perilously close to being a funeral wreath, becomes a "buoy," both a guide and a life jacket, once it becomes an individual gesture, not a gift that one pretends is for another. In a similar way, what a poem is must be reconceived: if it is supposed to be a present for others, an offering made as a self-sacrifice, it can only be rejected by the men at work on the stone wharf, who are quite certain who owns what, and for whom nothing else matters; the poem must be acknowledged by its poet, above all, not as a gift but as a personal impulse, as frail as a wreath, woven with affection, but of use primarily to its maker.

In his city poems, Merwin values the odd, quirky gestures he makes through them, accepting the helplessness of their gestures, but insisting on their rightness. Unlike the poems in the first third of the book, where the poet is constantly stymied, always trying to clarify a point, to niggle over a detail, to begin again to justify himself, these urban poems are full of declarations, insistences. In 1960, when expanding one of his short poems into "The Nails," his strategy was to add a refrain that undercut his previous words: "It isn't as simple as that." By contrast, in 1961, these city poems cut against such irresolution; he declares himself having arrived home, even as the essential rootlessness of the modern city reaffirms itself.

—Edward J. Brunner, *Poetry as Labor and Privelege: The Writings of W.S. Merwin* (Urbana: University of Illinois Press, 1991): pp. 124–125.

WORKS BY
W.S. Merwin

The Mask of Janus, 1952.

The Dancing Bears, 1954.

Green With Beasts, 1956.

The Poem of the Cid (trans.), 1959.

The Drunk in the Furnace, 1960.

The Satires of Perseus, 1961.

Spanish Ballads Translated with an Introduction, 1961.

The Moving Target, 1963.

Collected Poems, 1966.

Selected Translations, 1948–1968, 1968.

The Lice: Poems, 1969.

The Carrier of Ladders, 1970.

Signs, 1970.

The Miner's Pale Children, 1970.

Asian Figures, 1973.

Writings to an Unfinished Accompaniment, 1973.

The First Four Books of Poems, 1975.

The Compass Flower: Poems, 1977.

Houses and Travelers, 1977.

Sanskrit Love Poetry, trans. with J. Moussaieff Masson, 1977.

Feathers from the Hill, 1978.

The Peacock's Egg: Love Poems from Ancient India, trans. with
    J. Moussaieff Masson, 1981.

Finding the Islands, 1982.

Unframed Originals: Recollections by W.S. Merwin, 1982.

Opening the Hand: Poems, 1983.

Regions of Memory: Uncollected Prose, 1949–82. Eds. Ed Folsom
    and Cary Nelson, 1987.

The Rain in the Trees: Poems, 1988.

Selected Poems, 1988.

The Lost Upland, 1992.

Travels: Poems, 1993.

The Vixen: Poems, 1996.

Flower & Hand: Poems 1977–1983, 1996.

The Folding Cliffs: A Narrative, 1998.

East Window: The Asian Translations, 1998.

The River Sound: Poems, 1999.

The Pupil: Poems, 2001.

Sir Gawain and the Green Knight: A New Verse Translation, 2002.

W.S. Merwin

Bedient, Calvin. "Coloring Nature Big and Wet, Dry and Varied, and Pushed Aside." *The Antioch Review* 52 (Winter 1994): 15–33.

Bowers, Neal. "W.S. Merwin and Postmodern American Poetry." *The Sewanee Review* 98 (Spring 1990): 246–59.

Byers, Thomas B. *What I Cannot Say: Self, Word, and World in Whitman, Stevens, and Merwin.* Urbana: University of Illinois Press, 1989.

Carroll, Paul. *The Poem in Its Skin.* Big Table Books: 1968

Christhilf, Mark. *W.S. Merwin, The Mythmaker,* Columbia: University of Missouri Press, 1986.

——————. "Expressionist Imagery in the Poetry of W.S. Merwin." *The Midwest Quarterly* 27 (Spring 1986): 277–93.

Clifton, Michael. "Breaking the Glass: A Pattern of Visionary Imagery in W.S. Merwin." *Chicago Review* 36:1 (1988): 65–83.

Collins, Floyd. "A Poetry of Transcendence." *Gettysburg Review* 10 (Winter 1997): 683–701.

Cook, Albert. "Metrical Inventions: Zukofsky and Merwin," *College Literature* 24 (October 1997): 70–83.

Davis, Cheri. *W.S. Merwin,* Boston: Twayne, 1981.

Dunn, Stephen. "Poets, Poetry, and the Spiritual." *The Georgia Review* 52:2 (Summer 1998): 269–84.

Finley, Robert. "The Riddle's Charm." *Dalhousie Review* 77:3 (Autumn 1997): 313–22.

Frazier, Jane. "Writing Outside the Self: The Disembodied Narrators of W. S. Merwin." *Style* 30 (Summer 1996): 341–50.

Guy, Sandra M. "W.S. Merwin and the Primordial Elements: Mapping the Journey to Mythic Consciousness." *The Midwest Quarterly* 38 (Summer 1997): 414–23.

Hirsch, Edward. "The Art of Poetry XXXVIII: W.S. Merwin." *The Paris Review* 29 (Spring 1987): 57–81.

Hix, H.L. *Understanding W.S. Merwin*. Columbia: University of South Carolina Press, 1997.

Hoagland, Tony. "Body and Soul." *Gettysburg Review* 8 (Summer 1995): p. 505–22.

Hoeppner, Edward Haworth. *Echoes and Moving Fields: Structure and Subjectivity in the Poetry of W.S. Merwin and John Ashbery*. Lewisburg: Bucknell University Press, 1994.

——————. "A Nest of Bones: Transcendence, Topology, and the Theory of the Word in W.S. Merwin's Poetry." *Modern Language Quarterly* 49 (September 1988): 262–84.

——————. "Shadows and Glass: Mirrored Selves in the Poetry of W.S. Merwin and John Ashbery." *Philological Quarterly* 65 (Summer 1986): 311–34.

Nelson, Cary and Ed Folsom, eds. *W.S. Merwin: Essays on the Poetry*, Urbana: University of Illinois Press, 1987.

Revell, Donald. "A Counter-Language of Praise." *The Literary Review* 31 (Spring 1988): 363–6.

Sanderlin, Reed. "Merwin's 'The Drunk in the Furnace.'" *Contemporary Poetry* 2 (1975): 24–27.

Stiffler, Randall. "The Sea Poems of W.S. Merwin." *Modern Poetry Studies* 11: 3 (1983): 247–66.

Thomas, Michael W. "Merwin's For the Anniversary of My Death." *The Explicator* 49 (Winter 1991): 126–30.

Trengen, Linda and Gary Storhoff. "Order and Energy in Merwin's 'The Drunk in the Furnace.'" *Concerning Poetry* 13:1 (1980): 47–52.

ACKNOWLEDGMENTS

Alone With America: Essays on the Art of Poetry in the United States Since 1950 by Richard Howard: 433–434, 443–444. © 1980 by Richard Howard. Published by Atheneum. Reprinted by permission.

W.S. Merwin by Cheri Davis: 72–75, 98–103. © 1981 by G.K. Hall & Co. Reprinted by permission of the Gale Group.

"Merwin's Deconstructive Career" by Cary Nelson. From *W.S. Merwin: Essays on the Poetry,* edited by Cary Nelson and Ed Folsom: 88–91, 98–99, 104–105. © 1987 by the Board of Trustees of the University of Illinois. Reprinted by permission.

Poetry as Labor and Privilege: The Writings of W. S. Merwin by Edward J, Brunner: 85–86, 124–125, 142–143, 147–151. Copyright © 1991 by The University of Illinois. Reprinted by permission.

Understanding W.S. Merwin by H.L. Hix: 109–110. © 1997 University of South Carolina. Reprinted by permission.

W.S. Merwin the Mythmaker by Mark Christhilf, by permission of the University of Missouri Press: 28–30, 62–63. © 1986 by The Curators of the University of Missouri.

"Merwin and the Sorrows of Literary History" by Marjorie Perloff. From *W.S. Merwin: Essays on the Poetry,* edited by Cary Nelson and Ed Folsom: 132–137. © 1987 by the Board of Trustees of the University of Illinois. Reprinted by permission.

"Merwin's 'For the Anniversary of My Death'" by Michael W. Thomas. From the *Explicator* vol. 49, no. 2, Winter 1991: 126–129. Published by Heldref Publications, 1319 Eighteenth ST., NW, Washington, DC 20036-1802. © 1991 by Heldref Publications. Reprinted by permission.

INDEX OF
Themes and Ideas